Daily Promises
for
Women

Publications International, Ltd.

The Promise of Today

The word "promise" appears in our daily lives in so many ways. We promise to take out the garbage later or drive the kids to the movie theater. We see that an interesting thrift-store find has promise. Each new day promises both routines and surprises. But we may not realize the infinite promises God has given us for today, the rest of our lives, and all eternity.

The reality of being everyday women in a challenging world is that *only* when we are truly rested and peace-filled can we face life with steady optimism and joy, and make the most of opportunities that come our way. And it's *only* when we spend time in prayer—unloading our burdens and receiving God's rest and strength—that our hands are finally free to seize the good things God has promised to us.

Throughout the Bible, famous heroes and believers face trial after trial. There are famines and wars and plagues. But in the face of these obstacles, God promises to be there every time. "The adversaries of the Lord shall be broken to pieces; out of heaven shall he thunder upon them: the Lord shall judge the ends of the earth; and he shall give strength unto his king, and exalt the horn of his anointed" (1 Samuel 2:10).

So much of God's word is in that important future tense. God will break his enemies—our enemies—and protect those who believe and act in him. With his loving protection in our back pockets, we are freed to embrace the gift of life and make the most of each moment. How do we go about consistently taking hold of each day in a way that is meaningful and lasting?

Let *Daily Promises for Women* be your shining light. This volume of daily verses, prayers, and reflections will remind you to be thankful when times are flush and hopeful when things get hard. The verses and writings reflect a wide range of emotions, situations, and experiences—the ups and downs we encounter along the road of life. You'll discover a new favorite verse or revisit one you've lately overlooked.

The most wonderful feature of God's word is how it serves us all, regardless of who or where we are, who we know, or what we do. One reader's interpretation may vary from or even contradict that of someone else, but all roads lead to a better understanding of the path to the Lord. And if we better understand what God expects of us, we are better prepared to inherit the spiritual wealth contained in his promises.

In prayer, we unburden ourselves of the weight of the world, while receiving in return the "light yoke" of God's peace, his comfort, his very presence with us. As explained in 2 Corinthians 9:8, "God is able to make all grace abound toward you; that ye, always having all sufficiency in all things, may abound to every good work." He is here to support us, to free us to reach our full potential.

Daily Promises for Women puts the amazing power of God's word in your hands in an easy to read, inspiring format. Let our prayers and meditations touch off a conversation with God in your own life. What new promise will this day bring?

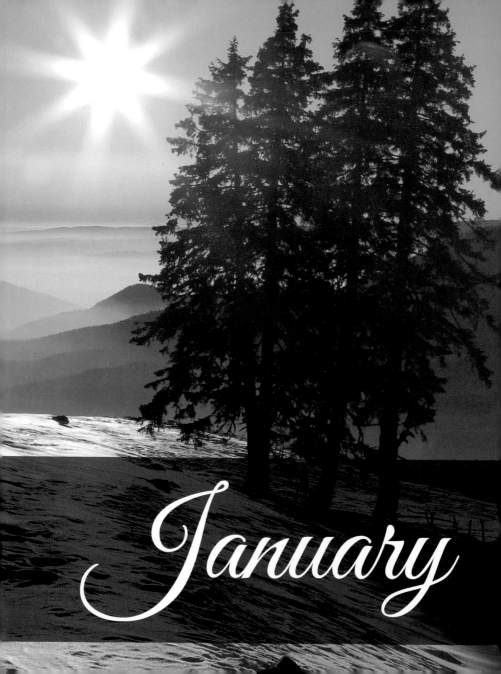

January

January 1

∞

And Ruth said, Intreat me not to leave thee, or to return from following after thee: for whither thou goest, I will go; and where thou lodgest, I will lodge: thy people shall be my people, and thy God my God. —Ruth 1:16

Children have the most amazing capacity for loyalty, God; they look to their parents with trust that all will be well. Lord, help me appreciate their trust as the privilege that it is. Help me to be a rock for my young ones, even as you are a rock for me. You see into my heart; you know the strength and fear that exist side by side within it. May you guide me—helping me access the strength I possess and the strength you give freely—as I strive to create a stable and loving home life for my family.

January 2

"The Lord bless him!" Naomi said to her daughter-in-law. "He has not stopped showing his kindness to the living and the dead." She added, "That man is our close relative; he is one of our guardian-redeemers." —Ruth 2:20

We are all connected, Lord, and may I impress upon my children the importance of this fact. Help me to demonstrate, not only in my words but also my actions, the fundamental role loving kindness should play in our lives. Whether it be aid to an injured animal, support and a listening ear to one who grieves, or respectful words spoken about someone who is deceased, may I put good into the world without expectation of recognition or reward. May I do good simply for the sake of doing good, and may I never stop showing kindness to those in need.

January 3

∞

And Joshua said unto them, "Fear not, nor be dismayed, be strong and of good courage: for thus shall the Lord do to all your enemies against whom ye fight."
—Joshua 10:25

Oh God, teach me to not fear adversity. Help me to accept and face challenges not only to myself but to my children. My kids will face unkindness; they will face unfairness, loss, and even cruelty in their life's journey. God, help me to remember that adversity breeds character—that we cannot necessarily control what happens to us but we can control our response to it. Grant me the strength to respond to adversity with grace, and please guide me as I give my children the tools to greet life's vicissitudes with faith in you, and with courage.

January 4

For in six days the Lord made heaven and earth, the sea, and all that in them is, and rested the seventh day: wherefore the Lord blessed the Sabbath day, and hallowed it. —**Exodus 20:11**

Lord, my days are so full that the pace of life can become frenetic. Regardless of the shape of my day, many people depend upon me to be cheerful and strong, from children to seniors, and it is sometimes difficult to remember to take care of myself. If I let them, my many responsibilities can overwhelm—even consume—me. May I always remember to rest and make time for You. Please help me to slow down and cultivate a peaceful heart.

January 5

∞

And the Lord passed by before him, and proclaimed, The Lord, The Lord God, merciful and gracious, longsuffering, and abundant in goodness and truth. —**Exodus 34:6**

Though each day I strive to be a positive role model and a loving mother, a wise and funny friend or daughter or spouse, I do not always live up to my potential. Thank you, Lord, for always being there with me, even on days when I am not at my best, and for your patience with my faults. Please guide me as I try to be the best person I can be; please help me to persevere even on the most difficult days, to remember that when I fail, you are always there to raise me up. Sustained by you, may I meet each day with an open heart and gracious spirit.

January 6

And now abideth faith, hope, charity, these three; but the greatest of these is charity. —**1 Corinthians 13:13**

I am infinitely blessed that in a world full of different people, you have chosen to give your heart to me. I am forever grateful that in a world full of different paths you have chosen to walk beside me. I am eternally joyful that in a world full of different opportunities you have chosen to create a life for me.

January 7

*Bear ye one another's burdens, and so fulfil
the law of Christ.* —Galatians 6:2

Marriage does not ask that you completely lose
yourself in the other person. Remember, happy individuals
make happy couples. Marriage does not demand that you
think and act just like one another. Remember, it was your
unique qualities that attracted you to each other in the
first place. Marriage only requires that each of you
becomes not someone else, but more of who you are
already, only now you will become who you are together.

January 8

Thou shalt not covet thy neighbour's house, thou shalt not covet thy neighbour's wife, nor his manservant, nor his maidservant, nor his ox, nor his ass, nor any thing that is thy neighbour's. —**Exodus 20:17**

God, we live in a materialistic society. Our society's values are skewed to the point where an individual might be judged worthy because of their possessions or the way they look, rather than by the grace they put into the world. In such an environment, it can be difficult to not envy those who have what society says is good. God, help me to recognize what is truly important in life. Help me to sort through the mixed messages one encounters every day, and to have gratitude for what really matters: health, adequate food and shelter, and the love, acceptance, and respect that are ultimately, truly earned—not from things, but from the way we live our lives.

January 9

Fear not, little flock; for it is your Father's good pleasure to give you the kingdom. —Luke 12:32

We can take a lesson from the precious water lily. For no matter what outside force or pressure is put upon the lily, it always rises back to the water's surface again to feel the nurturing sunlight upon its leaves and petals. We must be like the lily, steadfast and true in the face of every difficulty, that we too may rise above our problems and feel God's light upon our faces again.

January 10

In returning and rest shall ye be saved; in quietness and in confidence shall be your strength. —**Isaiah 30:15**

Most of us realize that we are naturally self centered, and we often respond to those around us in ways that make us appear proud, haughty, or arrogant. But if we look at Jesus' life, we see an excellent example of humility—an

example that we should strive to follow. He taught that pride was destructive, but humility was powerful. Rather than touting his own greatness, Jesus was willing to kneel down and wash the feet of others, to show that we should all be servants to each other—and to God.

January 11

∞

*And Moses cried unto the Lord, saying, "Heal her now, O God,
I beseech thee."* —Numbers 12:13

Lord, there are people I love who are burdened: their
hearts are burdened by sorrow, or they suffer serious
physical affliction. I have loved ones who are dying of
cancer, and what I want to pray is that they be healed,
completely. Help me to understand the many forms
"healing" can take, whether a complete restoration of
health, or an acceptance, an ability, to bear the cards life
has dealt. I pray for learned doctors and medicine that
effectively eases pain. I pray for strength of spirit—on the
part of the sufferer, but also on my part, that I might know
how best to offer comfort. Healing can take so many
forms; God, may your hands heal those in need.

January 12

The Lord bless thee, and keep thee. —**Numbers 6:24**

God, this morning my day started badly. My alarm didn't go off and I had to rush to get ready for work. It was raining and my hair was frizzy. My daughter has a cold and she was grumpy at breakfast. As we raced around the house we snapped at one another about silly things: how I prepared the toast, the fact that she didn't clear the table when she was done eating. I felt lonely in my foul temper! And yet when I drove my daughter to school the sun came out, and I saw again how beautiful she is, with her clear bright profile and her keen mind, and when we parted she told me she loved me. God, help me to remember and appreciate all the blessings you have given me. Help me to remember what is truly important, and that in your love we are never alone.

January 13

Call unto me, and I will answer thee, and show thee great and mighty things, which thou knowest not.

— Jeremiah 33:3

God, we know that pain has produced some wisdom in our lives, but it has also created cynicism and fear. People turn on us, reject us, hurt us, and none of us wants to play the fool more than once, so we're tempted to close off our hearts to people and to you. But relationships that bring meaning and joy require vulnerability. Help us trust you to be our truest friend and to lead us to the kind of community that will bring healing rather than destruction.

January 14

How precious also are thy thoughts unto me, O God! how great is the sum of them! —**Psalm 139:17**

This is not a choice I would make, for me or for the one who went against my standards, my hopes. It's a riddle, O God, why you give us freedom to choose. Comfort me as I cope with a choice not mine; forgive any role I had in it. Help me separate doer from deed as I pass on your words to all: "Nothing can separate us." Not even poor choices I sometimes make myself.

January 15

∞

This book of the law shall not depart out of thy mouth; but thou shalt meditate therein day and night, that thou mayest observe to do according to all that is written therein: for then thou shalt make thy way prosperous, and then thou shalt have good success. —Joshua 1:8

God, life offers so many distractions: so much freedom to do this and be that. This is inherently a good thing, but in the ceaseless flurry of information and opportunity it can be easy to lose one's way. I don't want to be a "deer in the headlights"; though I desire to be free and actively seek freedom of choice, I also crave direction in my life. Dear Lord, grant me a level head and an open heart. Help me to remember to keep your commandments as a touchstone, a way of being, so that no matter what else is going on in my life, I have a guide to follow. Keeping your commandments is a sure way to a successful life.

January 16

There shall not any man be able to stand before thee all the days of thy life: as I was with Moses, so I will be with thee: I will not fail thee, nor forsake thee. —**Joshua 1:5**

Thank you, God, for never forsaking me, whether times are good or bad. In my life I have encountered all manner of people: lifelong friends, false friends, family who comforted me in my cradle and then stood beside me as I grew. But life brings change again and again. Death might take our loved ones; fair-weather relationships might seem strong but fade in the face of adversity or simply with time. As I grow older, I sometimes fear change and the loss it can bring. Help me to remember that you are always there for me, a rock and a comfort all the days of my life.

January 17

In my distress I cried unto the Lord, and he heard me.

—Psalm 120:1

Of the many ways to suffer, I feel all of them in this firestorm of sadness. It robs my sleep, saps my strength, and changes me so much I hardly recognize myself. Ease my misery, Lord. Clear my mind as though washing streaks from a window. Hold me, releasing feelings that

keep me sick; send others to hold me, too. This pain is temporary and can be relieved, just like my worries.

January 18

For he shall give his angels charge over thee, to keep thee in all thy ways. They shall bear thee up in their hands, lest thou dash thy foot against a stone. —**Psalm 91:11–12**

Why tornadoes, Lord? Why typhoons or fires? Why floods or earthquakes? Why devastating accidents or acts of terror, Lord? It's so hard to understand. Perhaps there is no way to find any sense in overwhelming circumstances. Perhaps it's about trusting in you, God, no matter what comes and leaving it in your hands, where it belongs because, in fact, you do really love us and care about us and will make things work out for us.

January 19

He hath shewed thee, O man, what is good; and what doth the Lord require of thee, but to do justly, and to love mercy, and to walk humbly with thy God? —**Micah 6:8**

We have seen that inconceivable acts can cause our world to crumble around us. Yet we need not fall apart inside. If we place our trust in God's goodness, he will come to our aid and bring us comfort to restore our hope in the future. His love and compassion will lift our spirits so we can rejoice no matter what disaster or tragedy may befall us. For as long as God is beside us, nothing can defeat us or take what is truly important from us.

January 20

Now therefore so shalt thou say unto my servant David, thus saith the Lord of hosts, I took thee from the sheepcote, from following the sheep, to be ruler over my people, over Israel.

—2 Samuel 7:8

Lord, I have many roles in life. I am by turns a wife, a mother, a daughter, a sister, a friend, an employee. Some of my roles are informed by caregiving and it is an honor and a privilege to take care. Yet society does not always give as much attention or respect to those who care for others; caregiving can be an "invisible job," significant but not acknowledged in terms of the energy, love, and skill entailed. God, thank you for recognizing that each role I play matters. Thank you for reminding me that when I care for another I am living Christ's teachings. You take the most humble among us and lift us up in your glory.

January 21

∞

For I know the thoughts that I think toward you, saith the Lord, thoughts of peace, and not of evil, to give you an expected end. —**Jeremiah 29:11**

When a long-term relationship comes to an end, it's natural to mourn the loss of a companion and to grieve the death of a particular way of life. But we can mourn and grieve only for so long, then we must ask God to give us the grace and the courage to finally close that door and walk toward a new door waiting to be opened. We must take the next step God has for us. The more we seek the light, the brighter it becomes. This is God's love and compassion for us making itself known, and in his growing presence we become stronger and our faith is renewed.

January 22

Let not your heart be troubled: ye believe in God, believe also in me. In my Father's house are many mansions: if it were not so, I would have told you. I go to prepare a place for you.

—John 14:1-2

Blessed is the person who has steadfast and unmoving faith when everything is going wrong. That's when faith is most needed. If a person can look beyond the illusion of negative appearances and believe in a higher power at work, faith will move mountains and bring solutions.

January 23

∞

And David was afraid of the Lord that day, and said, "How shall the ark of the Lord come to me?" —2 Samuel 6:9

God, I made a mess of things today. I meant well: I leapt out of bed with a smile. But as the day progressed, I found myself losing equanimity. It was a long commute, and when someone cut me off I felt my temper rising. I had to change a lunch appointment; my friend expressed disappointment and at that point in the day, knee-deep in work, I felt too stressed to listen and respond with grace. Where was the calm, gracious person I was determined to be only this morning? And yet through it all, I know you love me. Thank you for always blessing me with your loving-kindness. Thank you for reminding me that, with you, there is always another chance to be our best selves.

January 24

And the angel of the Lord said unto Elijah, "Go down with him: be not afraid of him." And he arose, and went down with him unto the king. —**2 Kings 1:15**

As I strive to be a good role model for my children, I am reminded of how it can be easy to take "short cuts." Doing the right thing can be hard! This came home to me the other day when I was asked to visit an elderly relative in hospital. This person is very ill, and Lord, I have to admit: I was afraid. But I knew that the importance of the visit must needs eclipse my own fears, that it was the correct and Godly thing to do. Thank you for being there with me when I went to support another. Thank you for reminding me that it is never a mistake to do the right thing. May I never hesitate to obey you under any circumstance.

January 25

And the angel said unto them, Fear not: for, behold, I bring you good tidings of great joy, which shall be to all people.

—Luke 2:10

Joy reaches up in the middle of poverty to dance in the eye of a child at play. It spreads itself across the face of an old man whose illness is forgotten the moment he greets an old friend. Joy wedges itself through the cracks of loneliness when the voice at the other end of the phone line is that of someone familiar and loved. Joy is found

where it is least expected, because true joy roots itself not in the shifting sands of circumstance but in the rich soil of a grateful heart.

January 26

And I say unto you, Ask, and it shall be given you; seek, and ye shall find; knock, and it shall be opened unto you. For every one that asketh receiveth; and he that seeketh findeth; and to him that knocketh it shall be opened. —Luke 11:9-10

Once we've achieved inner balance and harmony, nothing external can disrupt that claim. People of faith who have true peace of mind know that they can meet both good fortune and misfortune with a positive attitude. Inner peace depends not on our circumstances but on how we choose to react to them.

January 27

Trust in the Lord with all thine heart; and lean not unto thine own understanding. —**Proverbs 3:5**

Sometimes I work so hard to control everything that I need to be reminded to take faith and "let go." Last night my head was in a whirl: I lay in bed and stared into the darkness, worrying about bills, my workload, if my son would ever get off the bench on his football team, if my husband and I would have time to care for the yard before the frost. It was only when I "let go" and decided to give my concerns over to you that I earned some measure of peace, and was able to sleep. Lord, thank you for your support and guidance as I navigate my busy days. May I have the faith to trust you over my own understanding.

January 28

The fear of the Lord is the beginning of knowledge: but fools despise wisdom and instruction. —**Proverbs 1:7**

God, my children are entering their teenage years, a time when they might think they know best and are immune to tutelage. How many times of late have they responded to my suggestions with impatience or even scorn? Help me to guide them with patience; to remind them, in love, of the importance of remaining open to instruction. May they keep your essence a grounding influence as they learn and grow, and may I remember that, old as I am, I, too, must always remain open to what you and the world have to teach me. We are never "done," are we? Lord, help me to keep my love of God at the center of my journey of learning and teach my children to do the same.

January 29

∞

Who can find a virtuous woman? For her price is far above rubies.
—Proverbs 31:10

What is virtue? To me, God, it is keeping a strong moral compass and adhering to a code of goodness despite the complexities of modern life. Life can be unfair. It can be cruel. We each have, every day, myriad excuses for not taking the high road: for exacting revenge, indulging in gossip, for harboring anger or hatred within our hearts. Lord, help me to stay the course; help my children and loved ones to navigate the world with grace and compassion. May hardship never dull our sense of what is correct, and may we meet our days with energy, joy, and a renewed sense of what it means to put grace into the world. God, help us to stand tall.

January 30

Now the Lord of peace himself give you peace always by all means. The Lord be with you all. —2 Thessalonians 3:16

The secret to happiness lies within the present moment. Only in the "here and now" will we find our life waiting to happen. Wise is the soul that cherishes this day, this moment, and doesn't long for others. Fortunate is the heart that loves what's in front of it, not what it wishes it had. And blessed is the mind that worries not over what was but focuses entirely on what is.

January 31

Therefore take no thought, saying, What shall we eat? or, What shall we drink? But seek ye first the kingdom of God, and his righteousness; and all these things shall be added unto you. —Matthew 6:31,33

By investing in yourself with faith and works, you improve your present and your future. So go ahead—volunteer to teach classes, take that mission trip, join a Bible study. Consult faith in your heart as you make choices with your life and your time and your way will be illuminated.

February

February 1

Keep thy heart with all diligence; for out of it are the issues of life. —**Proverbs 4:23**

God, we live in a fast-moving time. There are so many distractions; the very tools that help us navigate our days can also unhinge us. How many times have I interrupted my husband in service to an incoming call or text? How many times have I multitasked admirably, taking advantage of all that the digital world allows, but ignored the flesh-and-blood people with whom I shared a room? It is impossible to be present and listen fully when I have one eye on my phone. God, please help me to retain my priorities, to give the people I am with my full love and attention—my undivided self. May I always protect my heart and listen with my heart.

February 2

And above all things have fervent charity among yourselves: for charity shall cover the multitude of sins. —**1 Peter 4:8**

Tonight there was a shooting star but I couldn't see it. There was no trail against the deep dusk. And as I mused at what I'd seen, the other stars burned on. Some people, like shooting stars, are a wonderful presence that awakens our sleeping sense of adventure. Others are the stars that appear each night: always with us, faithful to the end.

February 3

Blessed is the man that walketh not in the counsel of the ungodly, nor standeth in the way of sinners, nor sitteth in the seat of the scornful. —Psalm 1:1

Kindness, compassion, and courtesy are contagious. Be true to your faith and values in your works. Wave a car ahead of you in traffic. Ask the supermarket checker about her day. Run errands for a sick friend. The language of an open and loving heart is heard in the quietest, most simple gestures.

February 4

∞

Every word of God is pure: He is a shield unto them that put their trust in him. —**Proverbs 30:5**

I have a friend who has read the Bible from cover to cover, and he described it as a profound experience. I have not read the Bible in this manner; I have favorite verses but, truth be told, biblical prose can be intimidating. I don't always understand how the verses apply to my leaky faucet or sick pet. There are so many interpretations of what lies within the Bible's pages! God, grant me a clear, level head and an open heart so that I might understand the wise ways of your word. May the rich stories, the adventures and drama and instruction that the Bible has to offer, be accessible to me. May I have the wisdom to apply its contents to my day-to-day life, and may I always be open to your teachings.

February 5

Iron sharpeneth iron; so a man sharpeneth the countenance of his friend.   **Proverbs 27:17**

Dear Lord, yesterday I had a peer review of a project I've worked on for months. The project is a good example of where I am in my creative journey. It is a personal expression of what I hold dear. The feedback was overall positive, but one peer in particular was especially blunt. I felt myself grow defensive and close my heart to her. It was only after I slept on it that I came to a reluctant conclusion: while her delivery was not diplomatic, and while I might not agree with all her suggestions, there was, in her commentary, a grain of truth. I recognized that some of her recommendations were in fact helpful, and that my work might benefit if I paid heed. God, help me to stay open to the instruction of others in my life.

February 6

For God sent not his Son into the world to condemn the world; but that the world through him might be saved. He that believeth on him is not condemned: but he that believeth not is condemned already, because he hath not believed in the name of the only begotten Son of God. —1 John 3:16–17

The love and devotion of family serves as the foundation upon which faith is built and cherished. The support of family acts both as wings to fly and a safety net to catch us. The honesty and trustworthiness of family creates both sanctuary and accountability for each of us in our journeys.

February 7

∞

Be perfect, be of good comfort, be of one mind, live in peace;
and the God of love and peace shall be with you.

—2 Corinthians 13:11

It sometimes takes a tragic event to open our eyes to the blessings that surround us, to show us the joy in life's simple moments. Our family, friends, our neighbors, and

our communities suddenly become havens of love, support, and comfort in the midst of tragedy. Wise is the person who can see the magic and wonder in simple things without having to suffer a great loss or disaster.

February 8

∞

Commit thy works unto the Lord, and thy thoughts shall be established. —**Proverbs 16:3**

God, having a small child inspires me to tap into a joyful, childlike view of the world. Today my daughter and I made a playhouse out of the box from our new oven. I cut out windows and a door; my little girl colored shutters in salmon and blue. Proceeding with great concentration, she happily drew flowers in pretend window boxes. Afterwards, we squeezed inside and sat on pillows, eating crackers and peanut butter. Oh Lord, the moment—the afternoon entire—seemed infused with your goodness, as if by the fact of our proceeding with a pure heart, the project itself was blessed. Thank you for this day. May everything I do, may every task I undertake, be likewise in your honor and made spiritual by your guidance.

February 9

Bless the Lord, ye his angels, that excel in strength, that do his commandments, hearkening unto the voice of his word.

—Psalm 103:20

God, I couldn't help noticing all the loveliness you placed in the world today! This morning I saw a sunrise that made my heart beat faster. I watched a father gently help his child across a busy parking lot; his tenderness was much like yours. I spied an elderly couple sitting on a bench. As the man told jokes, their laughter lifted my spirits. Later, I talked with a friend who aids needy families; her compassion inspired me. Thank you, Lord, for everything that is beautiful and good in the world.

February 10

In all things shewing thyself a pattern of good works: in doctrine shewing uncorruptness, gravity, sincerity, sound speech, that cannot be condemned. —**Titus 2:7-8**

Human beings are the only creatures that strive to be something they are not. We should take a lesson from the birds, who never ache to do anything but fly on a lifting breeze; or wild horses, who thunder over the open plains, never stopping to wish they were anything more than what God made them.

February 11

Pride goeth before destruction, and an haughty spirit before a fall. —**Proverbs 16:18**

God, may I not be blinded by pride. Sometimes, unrelated to our own efforts, we are visited by good things and times of prosperity. The longer I live, the more I recognize the inevitability of ups and downs in life: one following the other in unbroken succession all the days of our existence. May I never succumb to hubris and assume that I am exempt from challenge or entitled to times of prosperity. Lord, help me to ride the tide of life, wearing my accomplishments with grace and weathering any challenges with dignity. May I greet every day with gratitude, and may I always remember that you are with me, regardless of whether the day on its surface seems good or bad.

February 12

Be merciful unto me, O God, be merciful unto me: for my soul trusteth in thee: yea, in the shadow of thy wings will I make my refuge, until these calamities be overpast. —**Psalm 57:1**

Why does it seem impossible to wait patiently and graciously for an overdue phone call, a long-expected letter, an ailing loved one to get better? Is there a special ingredient to speed the passage of time and relieve my burdens? Lord, please teach me to wait and trust in you.

February 13

And they sing the song of Moses the servant of God, and the song of the Lamb, saying, Great and marvellous are thy works, Lord God Almighty; just and true are thy ways, thou King of saints —Revelation 15:3

I felt enchantment when my angel brushed my face with silken fingers. I felt empowered when my angel whispered forgiveness to my soul. I felt protected when my angel offered me shelter and lightness beneath her wings. I felt enlightened when my angel showed me how to reach for my dreams among the stars. In the Lord's flock I find strength and comfort.

February 14

∞

A soft answer turneth away wrath: but grievous words stir up anger. —**Proverbs 15:1**

Lord, what strength it can take to be kind! While it is easy to be nice to the nice, it is hard work to respond to unkindness with warmth and dignity. A sour woman at the grocery store snapped at me when she felt my cart was in her way. I apologized and moved the cart with a smile. She did not smile back and with effort I held my tongue. This minor incident reminded me that each situation demands a choice. God, help me to remember that I do not know what happens in the lives of others; their foul tempers may spring from grief or hardship, from hurts unseen. Remind me that when I react with anger, I only hurt myself. May I have the strength to answer anger with kindness, God. Help me to be firm but kind.

February 15

If the spirit of the ruler rise up against thee, leave not thy place; for yielding pacifieth great offences. —Ecclesiastes 10:4

*L*ord, we expect to learn that "life isn't fair," but when it hurts the most is when our loved ones experience misfortune or injustice. Sometimes we try to interfere and cushion the fall but they resist and must learn for themselves in their own time. Help me to yield to your will even when I think I see the clearest path for them, and help me to welcome them back with forgiving and open arms.

February 16

Therefore all things whatsoever ye would that men should do to you, do ye even so to them: for this is the law and the prophets. —**Matthew 7:12**

We are given our lights to let them shine, not to hide them or fear our pride. There is a godly way to express every talent and a charitable outlet for every gift! When we open our storehouse of talents and treasures, the whole world benefits and is made brighter by generous loving kindness. We honor God through our willingness to share with and enrich others.

February 17

He that spareth his rod hateth his son: but he that loveth him chasteneth him betimes. —**Proverbs 13:24**

My son doesn't like doing homework. It's hard for him—he struggles with academics and he'd rather be playing baseball, a sport at which he excels. God, I don't like conflict. And we can butt heads when I insist he complete his work before play: I have lost my temper on more than one occasion, frustrated because he needs to do the work and yet doesn't want to do the work. Frustrated because I don't like to fight with him. Sometimes I am tired and tempted to just let it go, though I know this would do him no favors. Dear God, help me to step up to the plate and be the adult I need to be. Please give me the strength to discipline my children when necessary, and help me to do so with love.

February 18

My flesh and my heart faileth: but God is the strength of my heart, and my portion for ever. —**Psalm 73:26**

ord, I confess I feel unduly burdened at times by this pain. Some days I can barely move, and some days my heart feels sick from the sadness. Let me move with ease and grace and walk in health again. Take this yoke upon you, Lord, and help me toward my goal. I long to be released from my illness and made whole again, made free to do my best work for you. If you can nudge me in the right direction, Lord, I'll take care of the rest.

February 19

For the fruit of the Spirit is in all goodness and righteousness and truth. —**Ephesians 5:9**

The mind is like a garden of fertile soil into which the seeds of our ideas and intentions are planted. With love and nurture, those seeds bloom forth to manifest in our lives as wonderful opportunities and events. Lord, please help me to plant fruitful seeds of goodness and light in my own life and those around me.

February 20

∞

Honour the Lord with thy substance, and with the firstfruits of all thine increase. —**Proverbs 3:9**

Dear Lord, I am blessed. Life can be difficult but it is also beautiful, and I am thankful that my husband and I have work even in difficult times. Our family has enough to eat; my children have friends who are good to them; we are healthy. In fact, good health gives me the energy to parent my children, to do the work I need to do, to support others—indeed, what are we here for if not to connect with and uplift those around us?—and to pursue what fulfills me. Yesterday I worked in the garden. The peppers are blooming and my cat dozed in the shade nearby. My heart was so full! God, thank you. Help me to remember gratitude, and may I always remember to honor you with everything I have.

February 21

Go to the ant, thou sluggard; consider her ways, and be wise.
—Proverbs 6:6

Lord, may I be alert to the teachings of all the creatures of nature that you have given us. I have two cats at home: like humans, each has its own temperament. One is playful, almost doglike; the other, more reserved, shows her love in quiet, unexpected ways. They like to be with us and gravitate to the rooms where we are working or playing. I find that to have a cat on my lap as I knit or write is a most comforting thing. I feel the rumbling as they purr. I sense their love and it gives me solace. Thank you for these creatures who remind me of the different ways one can be in the world. They ask for little and I am humble in the face of their unconditional love.

February 22

When he hath tried me, I shall come forth as gold. —**Job 23:10**

Heavenly Father, please help me realize there are different forms of healing. There are moments when life doesn't seem to change and I have to look inside to find a place of acceptance. It is in this place where I am reminded that who I am is separate from the pain that invades my life. Please help me to turn my thoughts to you. Amen.

February 23

And when we cried unto the Lord, he heard our voice, and sent an angel, and hath brought us forth out of Egypt.

—Numbers 20:16

My friend and I have had a falling out, Lord. The atmosphere is strained between us; the air is chilly. I don't know what I've said or done to cause this breach in our relationship. I only know we're at odds and my heart hurts. Relieve the anguish that I feel, Lord. Show me how to break the silence. Help me take the first step, then you can do the rest. Heal us with your love.

February 24

Behold, I send an Angel before thee, to keep thee in the way, and to bring thee into the place which I have prepared.

—Exodus 23:20

Lord, your forgiveness and love for me have transformed my life. I've been healed and liberated by fellowship and the chance to wipe the slate clean. Help me to become an extension of your love to those around me. Protect me as I learn to be vulnerable and to love my enemy as is your will. Please grant me strength. Amen.

February 25

∞

But let it be the hidden man of the heart, in that which is not corruptible, even the ornament of a meek and quiet spirit, which is in the sight of God of great price. —1 Peter 3:4

The seasons have meaning with our quiet loved ones.

In spring, we weed the beds and plant the flowers. In fall, we pick the peaches, apples, and berries. In winter, we bundle up in afghans before the fire, reading, sharing, and laughing, with bellies full of warming meals. When spring returns, daffodil bulbs poke up their shoots through softening earth. As we work together and nurture one another, our love grows.

February 26

Blessed be the Lord, who daily loadeth us with benefits, even the God of our salvation.—**Psalm 68:19**

The house is a mess, Lord, and because of it, my attitude is a matching mood. Like writing on the wall of my grumpy heart, I got your message: 'Tis far wiser to hunt first crocuses on spring days than lost socks in the laundry; to sweep leaves into piles for jumping than grunge in a corner; to chase giggles rising from a child's soul like dandelion fluff than dust balls beneath beds. Bless, O Lord, this wonderful mess, and send me out to play.

February 27

Therefore we are buried with him by baptism into death: that like as Christ was raised up from the dead by the glory of the Father, even so we also should walk in newness of life.

— Romans 6:4

Drawn like moths to flame, kids lead us new places. Guide me, pathfinding God, for I'm an aerialist leaping from bar to bar. For seconds, I'm holding neither old nor new: It's impossible to grasp a second bar while holding the first. Children grow and, with the wings we have wanted to give them, leave our homes to make their own rich lives. These changes can be difficult—disappointing, sad, or even scary. Help me teach my children to swing on their own bars; to have standards, goals, a living faith. Steady me as I help them soar and learn from their uncertain first movements.

February 28

Set your affection on things above, not on things on the earth.
—**Colossians 3:2**

There is no greater mystery than love, Lord of covenants and promises. We are especially in its presence on an anniversary. Bless those who live, day after day after ordinary day, within the fullness of lifelong love, surely one of life's greatest mysteries. Bless them as they honor their past, even while they create a future. Let us bow before their accomplishments, which are an inspiration and blessing to us all.

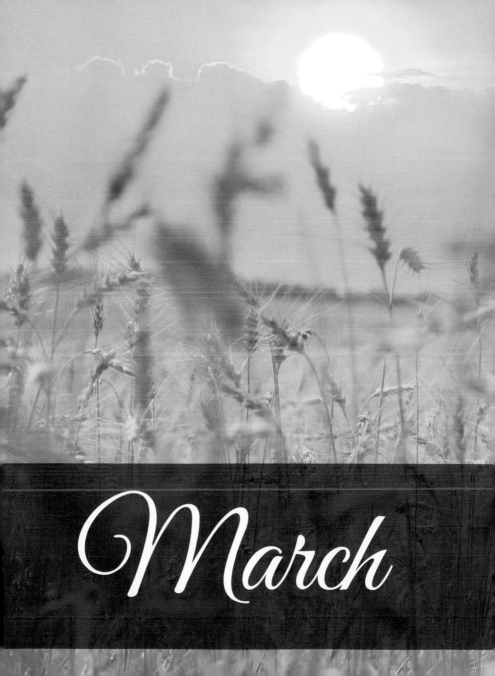

March

March 1

Give unto the Lord, ye kindreds of the people, give unto the Lord glory and strength. Give unto the Lord the glory due unto his name: bring an offering, and come before him: worship the Lord in the beauty of holiness.
—1 Chronicles 16:28-29, 34

Carpe diem—how's that for a motto, Lord? It invites me to forgive past errors, prioritize my to-do lists, and take steps today toward the rest of my life. What will endure? Time I gave the committees instead of family and self? Chores I did instead of picnicking, listening to a child's story, resting by a winding stream? Lord, your word inspires me not only to seize the day but to cherish it. Thank you for seeing the good in me and helping me to realize it.

March 2

But as for me and my house, we will serve the Lord.

—Joshua 24:15

My mom loves roses, probably because her mom loved roses. She cares for them in her garden, weeding, pruning, and enjoying their beautiful petals and fragrance. Lord, you guide my life and love me in the same way. I feel your hand leading me toward healthy and wise choices, toward mindfulness and charity. Help me to face the sun each day as my most redolent self. Amen.

March 3

But Jesus said, Suffer little children, and forbid them not, to come unto me: for of such is the kingdom of heaven.

—Matthew 19:14

Our hearts are glad when we see a new child for the first time, whether our own or those of our loved ones. We smile toward a distant destination in our minds. We bend to them, reaching a finger toward their miraculously tiny hands, their downy hair, all these hallmarks of God's creation. Thank you, Lord, for our beautiful children, challenging and vibrant in your image.

March 4

I am the good shepherd, and know my sheep, and am known of mine. —**John 10:14**

Our parents are wonderful; they are kids at heart. They tag along as we explore, hold the shells and "pretty rocks" we just have to keep, tell us jokes and laugh with us. It is one thing to talk about our connection to all living things but it is quite another to live it. Our parents sing us to sleep on hot summer nights and hold our hands as we walk unsteady paths. Bless our parents now and forever.

March 5

For my thoughts are not your thoughts, neither are your ways my ways, saith the Lord. For as the heavens are higher than the earth, so are my ways higher than your ways, and my thoughts than your thoughts. —**Isaiah 55:8–9**

Are you here, Lord? I've never felt lonelier than I do in this illness. When I despair, I repeat a child's prayer or familiar verse and feel soothed to connect with you. The act of praying reminds me of your presence in both sickness and health. Please help me to hold my head high so I may always feel the light of your love on my face, even in my darkest times.

March 6

God is faithful, who will not suffer you to be tempted above that ye are able; but will with the temptation also make a way to escape, that ye may be able to bear it. —1 Corinthians 10:13

I never meant to be a failure, Lord, never meant to break commitments, but I am and I did. Please comfort me, for I mourn this failure and its repercussions to my loved ones. I mourn for the person I pledged to be. Forgive my failures and help me to forgive myself and move on with courage. Help me grieve and move on from these toxic feelings.

March 7

The Lord thy God shall bless thee in all thy works, and in all that thou puttest thine hand unto. —**Deuteronomy 15:10**

Bless this candle-lit festival of birthday celebration, Lord, for our special loved one. Join us as we blow out candles and joke about setting the cake ablaze, about golden ages and silver hairs. Our laughter is bubbling up from gratitude that the years are only enriching this special celebrant. We are grateful that the years are also enriching our lives as friends and family as well, for we are the ones receiving the best birthday gift today: the gift of knowing this special person. Thank you for sharing.

March 8

Seeing ye have purified your souls in obeying the truth through the Spirit unto unfeigned love of the brethren, see that ye love one another with a pure heart fervently. —1 Peter 1:22

Welcome to our party, Lord of water-into-wine feastings. Stand with us as we honor our special loved ones on this great occasion. Be with us, their friends and family, as we share a meal, a memory, and a toast to each other. Be present at their daily table as you are with them around this festive banquet now. On every occasion, Lord, you are the true reason for celebration.

March 9

Beloved, if God so loved us, we ought also to love one another.
—1 John 4:11

Please join us, Lord, to honor the grandparents who tended us so well. Pause with us as we play again in the dusty lanes of childhood at Grandma and Grandpa's house. Bless these larger-than-life companions who helped us bridge home and away, childhood and maturity. In their footsteps, we made the journey. Thank you for such a heritage. We express our gratitude to you.

March 10

Put them in mind to be subject to principalities and powers, to obey magistrates, to be ready to every good work, to speak evil of no man, to be no brawlers, but gentle, shewing all meekness unto all men. —**Titus 3:1–2**

What more can I say, dear God, than I've said since before my beloved newly adult child was born? Watch over and visit this young person with your presence. We've done a pretty good job so far, you and I. And now it's time to let go. Be with me. I'm better at roots than wings. Remind me that nothing can separate us from one another or your love. Help me be there for my children as you are for me, companion God. Go with this child today. I mustn't follow too closely, and I can't yet judge my distance.

March 11

He that covereth a transgression seeketh love; but he that repeateth a matter separateth very friends. —**Proverbs 17:9**

No matter how hard I try, God of patience and support, someone finds fault with me. I am mortified about the latest criticism. Give me the courage to confront this, Lord, for it is not acceptable to be treated this way even when in error. Keep me calm, factual, and open; perhaps the tone was unintentional, the critic unaware of the power of shaming. Help me remember how I feel now the next time I find fault with someone. Truth be known, Lord, such abrasive manners say more about the criticizer than the criticized. Keep me from passing them on.

March 12

∞

A new heart also will I give you, and a new spirit will I put within you: and I will take away the stony heart out of your flesh, and I will give you an heart of flesh. —Ezekiel 36:26

My heart is at home. Where better to think of you, Lord, than at home? It is where we have our history, begin our traditions, take our rites of passage. It is where we are first loved, first safe, first found to be special. It is where we are sheltered and nourished, then equipped and sent on our way. Throughout it all, you sit invisibly in our midst, blessing our spaces. Help us to always see the beauty, the opportunities in them. Bless us, the homebodies.

March 13

Do all things without murmurings and disputings: That ye may be blameless and harmless, the sons of God, without rebuke, in the midst of a crooked and perverse nation, among whom ye shine as lights in the world. —**Philippians 2:14–15**

Once the kids arrive, romance gets nudged aside by the carpool, and candlelit dinners happen only when the power is out. Which, we fear, God of love, could happen to us, the couple who were lovebirds once upon a time. Help us retrieve the "us" that supports the family, for we are a union blessed by you. As we cope with a full house now, remind us of empty nests ahead, a love-nest time just for us. Remind us to take a minute for ourselves amidst the loving chaos of family life.

March 14

∞

And God said, This is the token of the covenant which I make between me and you and every living creature that is with you, for perpetual generations: I do set my bow in the cloud, and it shall be for a token of a covenant between me and the earth. —**Genesis 9:12-13**

In the final throes of winter, God of springtimes, I'm gardening. Carrot tops rooting, sweet potatoes vining. I don't doubt the outcome since I've learned at your knee to live as if. As if useless can become useful; as if seemingly dead can live; as if spring will come. How does a winter garden grow? With hope. It grows brighter each time I live as if, knowing that you, O God, color even our wintry days from love's spring palette.

March 15

Hope deferred maketh the heart sick: but when the desire cometh, it is a tree of life. —**Proverbs 13:12**

We all know the sting of being heartsick. Loss, unrequited love, unfulfilled expectations—any of these can lead to the feeling of our heart literally being sick. The passage above tells us that it is actually deferring, or putting off, hope that truly makes our hearts sick. God knows the pain we experience in this life. He knows how to comfort us. If we cling to hope and turn to God, despite all that life may throw at us, we are sure to find ourselves filled with peace and joy.

March 16

He will swallow up death in victory; and the Lord God will wipe away tears from off all faces. —Isaiah 25:8

May your thoughts focus much more upon what you have than what you lack in this trying time. May your heart lay hold of present realities rather than future possibilities. For *this* moment, the now, is all we are given. Whether we are sick or healthy, this juncture in time is the place we share. Let us be blessed, needing nothing to change. Let us simply be in God's presence, just for this moment.

March 17

That the communication of thy faith may become effectual by the acknowledging of every good thing which is in you in Christ Jesus. —**Philemon 1:6**

Blessings upon you. The blessing of perfect acceptance in the face of daunting circumstances. The blessing of contentment and peace while the winds blow and the waves rise higher and higher. The blessing of knowing when acceptance must turn to action for the sake of all concerned. The blessing of strength to forsake contentment and peace for the purpose of comforting another. The blessing of discernment: to recognize when to wait, and to know when to move.

March 18

For every creature of God is good, and nothing to be refused, if it be received with thanksgiving: For it is sanctified by the word of God and prayer. —1 Timothy 4:4-5

Lord, being in love is a magical gift. Everything seems brighter and sharper in focus. My heart soars and my spirit is light as air, and all because of the love of another. But help me to also seek that deeper, more lasting love that comes from truly knowing another, even when the fires of passion become a gentle and steady simmer. Let love always be in my life, no matter what form it comes in.

Love of any kind is a magical gift. Thank you, Lord.

March 19

The Lord is thy keeper: the Lord is thy shade upon thy right hand. The sun shall not smite thee by day, nor the moon by night.

—Psalm 121:5-6

*L*ord, let my light shine brightly, even if it makes me feel uncomfortable. I am not used to standing in the spotlight. But you have convinced me that there is nothing wrong with feeling the love of who I am in your eyes, so help me get over the feeling of embarrassment and let my talents and gifts reveal themselves. There is no pride in letting the lamp of love you have lit within me give forth its glorious light. Show me how to enlighten the world and yet stay humble and grateful and true.

March 20

Rejoice evermore. Pray without ceasing. In every thing give
thanks: for this is the will of God in Christ Jesus concerning you.
—1 Thessalonians 5:16–18

God, the blessed feeling of being at home in your loving presence is like nothing else. The joy I feel when I know I never walk alone is the greatest of gifts, and when I look around at the wonderful people you have chosen to walk with me through life—my family and my friends—I truly know that I am loved. Thank you, God, for these miracles, these blessings, far too numerous to count. And to think I never have to look too far from home to find them is the best miracle of all.

March 21

Although the fig tree shall not blossom, neither shall fruit be in the vines; the labour of the olive shall fail, and the fields shall yield no meat; the flock shall be cut off from the fold, and there shall be no herd in the stalls: Yet I will rejoice in the Lord, I will joy in the God of my salvation.

—Habakkuk 3:17-18

Life is not easy; in fact, some days, even arising to face the day is a truly daunting task. Because sin entered the world and corrupted God's perfect design, we may find ourselves bruised like fragile reeds by the painful effects of a broken world. If we allow ourselves to stay in our broken state without relying on the powerful source of God's comfort, peace, and love, we might even find ourselves as hopeless as a smoldering wick about to lose its flame.

March 22

O Lord my God, I cried unto thee, and thou hast healed me.
—Psalm 30:2

The state of hopelessness is dangerous; it is one of the worst places to allow ourselves to dwell. However, God knows our heartache, and he understands our suffering. When we have been bruised in this world, he offers us healing. We may never understand why we have to encounter heartbreaking experiences, but we can hold securely to the truth that God's justice is certain. He will heat our hearts with the flame of his joy again.

March 23

For this shall every one that is godly pray unto thee in a time when thou mayest be found: surely in the floods of great waters they shall not come nigh unto him.
—Psalm 32:5

An honest man is not a man who never lies. There is no such man. When an honest man is caught in a lie or discovers he has lied, he is quick to admit it. He then speaks the truth. He's not afraid to say, "Please forgive me for not being honest." He does not defend a lie. Unlike a dishonest man, he does not make plans to lie or use lies to cover other falsehoods. He regularly scrutinizes his life to see if he has lied or is living a lie in any area. Honesty with God, his fellow man, and himself is the honest man's goal and his heart's desire.

March 24

And he believed in the Lord; and he counted it to him for righteousness.

—Genesis 15:6

We need to pass on to our children and remind ourselves that if we have deep convictions—convictions that have not just been handed to us, but that have been seared into our souls through difficult battles won—those convictions will be tested. They will be tried in the fires of outside pressures. I am not certain that a conviction is a worthwhile one if it is not tested and tried in the refining fires of life experiences and human opposition.

March 25

For the Lord God will help me; therefore shall I not be confounded: therefore have I set my face like a flint, and I know that I shall not be ashamed.

—Isaiah 50:7

There are many events in our lives over which we have no control. However, we do have a choice either to endure trying times and press on or to give up. The secret of survival, whether or not we question God's presence or his ability to help us, is remembering that our hope is in the fairness, goodness, and justice of God. When we put our trust in the character of a God who cannot fail us, we will remain faithful. Our trust and faithfulness produce the endurance that sees us through the "tough stuff" we all face in this life.

March 26

Wherefore, my beloved brethren, let every man be swift to hear, slow to speak, slow to wrath: For the wrath of man worketh not the righteousness of God.

—James 1:19–20

God, as much as I don't want to, I can't help but listen to your love, which calls me to always seek to make my enemies my friends. How I have grown to truly dislike the call of this love! I would rather love a stranger than an enemy. This is not easy to even want to do! Still, I know that this is what you want me to do in order to make your love real in my life. And so, Lord, flood me with your love because this call is a hard one for me. Amen.

March 27

Nay, in all these things we are more than conquerors through him that loved us.

—Romans 8:37

Lord, I'm looking forward to this new phase of my life. It is full of promise and hope, though I know that challenges will surely come as well. I know you have all the courage, strength, faithfulness, and love I need to meet each moment from a perspective of peace. I just need to stay tethered to you in prayer, listening for your Spirit to guide me and turn my thoughts continually back toward you. That's the key to a good life.

March 28

A man's pride shall bring him low: but honour shall uphold the humble in spirit.

—Proverbs 29:23

Ready or not, free time is at hand for some of your finest seasoned workers, Lord, early retirees downsized, outgrown, and prematurely put out to pasture. Help us start again, for we are hidden treasures other companies could use. Remind us as we start the search that even temporary employment is better than sitting around. Keep us in the workforce, for we, like fine furniture, gain luster with age, something young folks can't begin to match.

March 29

Be ye mindful always of his covenant; the word which he commanded to a thousand generations.

—1 Chronicles 16:15

May you know that a wisdom and a love transcend the things you will see and touch today. Walk in this light each step of the way. Never forget that there is more to this existence than the material side of things. And be blessed when you suddenly become aware of it: in the smile of a child, in the recognition of your own soul's existence, in the dread of death, and in the longing for eternal life.

March 30

Happy is he that hath the God of Jacob for his help, whose hope is in the Lord his God. Which made heaven, and earth, the sea, and all that therein is: which keepeth truth for ever.

Psalm 146:5 6

Bless our work, Lord of vineyards and seas. We yearn to be connected with what we do and to do something that matters. Show us that what we do is as indelible as a handprint on fresh concrete even though our mark may be in spots no one can see right now except us. Bless our left-behind marks, for with you as our foundation, our work is as essential to the overall structure of life as a concrete pillar.

March 31

Beareth all things, believeth all things, hopeth all things, endureth all things. —1 Corinthians 13:7

May you fall in love with this new family more and more each day. No, you weren't planning to suddenly have children, but here they are—a gift from your new spouse. A stepparent isn't accepted right from the start, so be patient. Love  will grow between you as you look out for one another's inner needs. Blessings upon you and the children. God grant that you be all a family can be.

April 1

∞

Now faith is the substance of things hoped for, the evidence of things not seen. —**Hebrews 11:1**

My heavenly Father, what do I have to fear when you are the one caring for me? And yet, I do fear; irrationally I fear, despite your faithfulness, despite your assurances, and despite your promises. I don't always understand my trembling heart and the shadows of things far smaller than you before which it cowers. Please liberate me from these lapses of trust. Let me stand fearlessly, supported by faith and hope, in the center of your love.

April 2

As the apple tree among the trees of the wood, so is my beloved among the sons. I sat down under his shadow with great delight, and his fruit was sweet to my taste.

—Song of Solomon 2:3

Dear God, I am lucky to have a soulmate. One must be strong and able to be happy alone, of course, but it's a profound comfort to have a partner with whom I can share joys and hardships. My husband and I have been together many years now, and we have grown together in love, trust, and tenacity. Being strong for one another has given us each courage. We support one another as individuals and together. And I enjoy his company! I feel lucky, Lord. My husband is a gift, and I praise you for this blessing.

April 3

∞

For, lo, the winter is past, the rain is over and gone.

—Song of Solomon 2:11

Lord, the longer I live, the more I realize that life is change. Help me to remember that even when times are hard, there will always be better times to come. Help me to understand, too, that sometimes what appears to be "bad" holds the seeds of good. When I did not get the job I wanted, I was inspired to apply for a job that was, in fact, better for me and for my family. God, grant me the patience to see how things unfold, and the wisdom to make the most of the opportunities I have.

April 4

The flowers appear on the earth; the time of the singing of birds is come, and the voice of the turtle is heard in our land.

—Song of Solomon 2.12

Dear God, my grandfather always used to say that nature was his church. He was a church-going man but he felt closest to you when he worked in the woods. I didn't understand that when I was a child but I understand it now: I have my best conversations with you when I am in nature. Nature's beauty is a balm; my heart becomes quiet and receptive. Oh God, every day there is a blessing in the earth you made, if I am willing to look for your presence in nature.

April 5

∞

And ye shall seek me, and find me, when ye shall search for me with all your heart. —**Jeremiah 29:13**

God, today I am mired in the challenges that life can bring. My mother is losing her battle with cancer. I try to be strong and supportive—for Mom as well as for my children—but inside I feel such fear. What will I do without her? How will I help my daughters navigate this loss? I know that you are there, but I feel depleted and alone, Lord. I do not always have the strength to seek you out. Please embolden my heart to always beckon for you.

April 6

Behold, ye trust in lying words, that cannot profit.
—Jeremiah 7:8

God, our world is full of false prophets who deceive with their charisma. Advertisements extol products that make us more beautiful or successful. Happier. There are people out there who might bring real harm to those I love. Lord, help me to guide my young ones so that they are wise without being hardened, that they might function in the world and not fall prey, but still retain their youthful hearts—their childhoods. Protect my young ones from deceit. It can break our hearts.

April 7

∞

The Lord is good, a strong hold in the day of trouble; and He knoweth them that trust in Him. —**Nahum 1:7**

*L*ord, yesterday my daughter came home from school consumed with worry. She had to study for a test and prepare for a recital. She and a friend were quarrelling. We talked about things she might do for herself and that other things must be given over to faith. I reassured her that no matter what happens in the days to come, you are always there for us, then smiled to realize that this is advice I might heed for myself! God, life is full of troubles and crises, and yet we take comfort that you are a refuge come what may.

April 8

∞

And Jesus came and spake unto them, saying, "All power is given unto me in heaven and in earth." —Matthew 28:18

God, I relate to Jesus. He walked the earth; he experienced fear and injustice and challenge. Yesterday I had to work with a combative and self-aggrandizing colleague, and I felt frustration and uncertainty. As I struggled to maintain a spirit of collaboration, I thought about Christ's messages of faith and compassion; though Jesus is your son, he didn't preach from an ivory tower. God, that fact brings solace even as it leaves me feeling in awe. Jesus is more than a teacher. He is your son. Thank you for giving us the gift of his teachings.

April 9

Think not that I am come to destroy the law, or the prophets: I am not come to destroy, but to fulfill. —**Matthew 5:17**

Dear God, in my efforts to forge my own best path and be a role model, may I always respect those who raised children before me. May I not challenge convention simply for the sake of doing so, and may I always do so with respect and propriety. Lord, please keep me mindful of the example Jesus set: to respect his elders and ancestors. He did not come to destroy their ways but to better them.

April 10

Not every one that saith unto me, Lord, Lord, shall enter into the kingdom of heaven; but he that doeth the will of my Father which is in heaven.

—Matthew 7:21

Lord, my father was a spiritual man, not always because of what he said but because of his actions. Everything he did, whether he was making bookshelves or helping us with our math, he did with love and mindfulness. Dad's life of quiet service—he never called attention to the caring things he did—was such a direct application of Christ's teachings. My father died years ago and I miss him every day. God, please help me to carry on what Dad personified; help me to remember that saying words of glory and praise is not the same as doing your will.

April 11

∞

Ye are the light of the world. A city that is set on an hill cannot be hid. —Matthew 5:14

Lord, there are times when one's inner well runs dry; we need periods of solitude to replenish, to connect with ourselves and with you, and to quiet our minds. But God, I do believe that we are here on this earth to associate with others and to help one another: help me to remember the importance of staying connected. Supporting one another gives life meaning. There are times when I want to retreat and be alone, but I cannot be a light to others in isolation. May you strengthen me to return from periods of solitude to be a light for you.

April 12

Lay not up for yourselves treasures upon earth, where moth and rust doth corrupt, and where thieves break through and steal. —Matthew 6:19

Dear Lord, last week a neighbor's home burned to the ground. Someone left a lit candle unattended, the drapes caught, and the old wooden house went down in flames. It was a fearsome event, but firefighters saved everyone in the house, even the family's two dogs. That's what the family members kept commenting on: not their lost possessions, but the fact that they were all alive. God, the event opened my eyes. I've become connected to the possessions that accumulate in my home, but they can be lost in a blink of an eye. Only your treasures of the heart and spirit will endure.

April 13

Moreover if thy brother shall trespass against thee, go and tell him his fault between thee and him alone: if he shall hear thee, thou hast gained thy brother. —**Matthew 18:15**

Dear Lord, I hate conflict. It is tempting to let conflicts fester and, instead, complain about the offender to others. It never makes me feel good; "venting" does little to

resolve a problem. God, grant me the wisdom to understand when it is time to confront, and help me to do so with grace. Confronting others is so difficult, and yet you have outlined the way to do it! Please give me the strength to resolve conflict firmly but discreetly.

April 14

∞

Judge not, that ye be not judged. —Matthew 7:1

Dear Lord, I have a daughter in middle school. She and her friends are coming into their own, trying to figure out who they are. Technology makes it even simpler to be unkind, and it is tempting to adopt a judgmental attitude in order to fit in with others. God, help me guide my children as they navigate this time of change and growth. Please protect my family from the ways of the judgmental, and from adopting those ways in their interactions with others.

April 15

∞

Then was Jesus led up of the Spirit into the wilderness to be tempted of the devil. —**Matthew 4:1**

Lord, I fell short today, and I'm sorry. I went to lunch with work colleagues and we gossiped about our boss, who is rumored to be on the brink of divorce. We were all so eager to contribute to the speculation, myself included, and in the moment I felt included and empowered. Afterward I felt ashamed. Every day brings its challenges, and we are constantly invited to be our best selves. God, it is no sin to be tempted: tempted to judge, tempted to gossip, tempted to deceive. It is what we do with that temptation that matters.

April 16

Take heed that ye do not your alms before men, to be seen of them: otherwise ye have no reward of your Father which is in heaven. —**Matthew 6:1**

The other day I caught myself mentioning my charitable giving to impress a new friend I'd met at work. I hardly know this woman and wanted her to like me. Better I should have expended that energy helping out at the shelter itself—giving of myself rather than talking about it! Lord, reaching out and supporting others is an act of pure love and service; may I always do so humbly and not to gain goodwill and praise. Please grant me humility.

April 17

And he said to them all, "If any man will come after me, let him deny himself, and take up his cross daily, and follow me."
—Luke 9:23

I had a cute poster in my childhood room that read, "It is hard to be good." All these years later, I remember the message! I didn't want to take my great aunt to the doctor last week, and would rather have stayed home to paint. Much to her chagrin, I counseled my youngest to honor a commitment she'd made to a friend even though a "better" invitation came along. God, service comes at a price; it can feel inconvenient or painful. May I follow you even when it seems difficult or inconvenient to do so.

April 18

Is any thing too hard for the Lord? At the time appointed I will return unto thee, according to the time of life, and Sarah shall have a son. —**Genesis 18:14**

Try to imagine Sarah's long wait for the heir God promised her husband, Abraham— music to the childless woman's ears—25 years during which her age began to make her doubtful. Sarah came up with a stopgap solution by securing for Abraham a second wife. Apparently, she figured God was going to need her help with this one. But it wasn't until the situation seemed completely impossible that the timing was just right for God to act. No one would ever doubt now that Isaac was a gift from his hand. Will God keep his promises to us? Absolutely! But maybe not like we imagined and sometimes even in ways that will tickle us pink.

April 19

*But I say unto you which hear, "Love your enemies, do good to them which hate you." —**Luke 6:27***

$\mathcal{D}$ear Lord, last year my son was bullied at school. The bully's parents were very difficult to work with and would not admit that their own son was at fault. My son got some relief when his class moved up a grade and went to different classrooms—he is fine, but when I see the bully's mother in town or at school, I am not. God, I know I need to release this bitterness. My heart needs to love, for hating only hurts the soul. Please help me to forgive those who have harmed me or those I love.

April 20

Shall not the Judge of all the earth do right? —**Genesis 18:25**

There are times when we feel God missed a beat in caring for us. We experience a painful loss, a cruel injustice, a terrible consequence of someone else's actions. Why didn't the Lord intervene? We must wrestle with this question: Will I still trust God? Abraham trusted God's goodness even when circumstances looked grim. He knew God would bring evil to account. He also knew God's merciful heart toward those who trust him. The Judge of all the earth has promised he will right all wrongs.

April 21

For with God nothing shall be impossible. —**Luke 1:37**

I am enduring a dark period, Lord. My beloved father is ravaged by Parkinson's disease, and I must assist him and my mother while I try to raise my own three children with strength, patience, and joy. Some nights I lie awake, filled with fear that my little family will not survive this next chapter—one of many "Sandwich Generation" families with children and parents to care for. Dear God, help me remain faithful to the promise that with you, nothing is impossible, even if I can't see through it myself.

April 22

For the Lord thy God hath blessed thee in all the works of thy hand: he knoweth thy walking through this great wilderness: these forty years the Lord thy God hath been with thee; thou hast lacked nothing.—**Deuteronomy 2:7**

God pledged to carry his people, Israel, safely to the land he promised to Abraham. After the promise was fulfilled, God wanted the people to review their experience. It wasn't because God needed a pat on the back. It was because he wanted his people to remember that they could always trust him to provide for their needs, that they could call on him and he would hear and respond.

April 23

But ye shall receive power, after that the Holy Ghost is come upon you: and ye shall be witnesses unto me both in Jerusalem, and in all Judaea, and in Samaria, and unto the uttermost part of the earth. —**Acts 1:8**

I call them my "blue days": when the demands of life deplete me. On these days it's hard to imagine that I can do all the things I need to do: work, cook, clean, weed the backyard, help my son with math and my daughter to untangle a thorny problem with a friend. I feel distracted and out of sorts. You feel far away. God, help me to remember that you fill your believers with power. Help me to tap into that power so I may stride into the world with energy, purpose, and joy. Thank you for your spirit every day, especially on days when I am down.

April 24

Know therefore that the Lord thy God, he is God, the faithful God, which keepeth covenant and mercy with them that love him and keep his commandments to a thousand generations.

—Deuteronomy 7:9

God is eager to bless those who draw near to him through his covenant of mercy, which is now offered to us through Christ's atoning sacrifice. It's interesting in light of this verse the perspective of some that God is distant, indifferent, angry, or ready to punish. Our notions about God can sometimes be so far away from the reality.

April 25

And the multitude of them that believed were of one heart and of one soul: neither said any of them that ought of the things which he possessed was his own; but they had all things common. —Acts 4:32

My daughter is learning about traditional Native American societies at school. The communal culture impressed her: sharing and giving were prized over personal possessions. She sparked a mindful discussion about the way possessions can take on undue importance. God, other cultures make a point of sharing, but the practice does not always come naturally in our modern world. Please help me to teach my children to share and give freely—and may my own actions also reflect and reinforce these principles.

April 26

∞

Them that honour me I will honour, and they that despise me shall be lightly esteemed. — 1 Samuel 2:30

Throughout the Bible, God repeatedly says that he resists the proud but exalts the humble. When we honor him, he responds to us in kind. While God has no interest in grinding us into subservience, humility is the gateway through which even Jesus entered to do his work on earth. In fact, our heavenly father's goal is to share all that he has with us, granting us life as co-heirs with Christ. It's counterintuitive to the world's way of thinking, but through humble respect and love—not arrogance—that we will inherit true greatness in God's kingdom.

April 27

Now faith is the substance of things hoped for, the evidence of things not seen. —**Hebrews 11:1**

Life is filled with uncertainty. Even wonderful news can cause stress, and we are called upon again and again in our lives to respond with grace. I worry, usually late at night. Will I be able to handle it? God, I know not what is around the corner in my life, and yet I need faith to believe in you regardless of what I cannot see. Please help me to remember that I can handle whatever lies ahead, good or ill, because you are always with me.

April 28

∞

*And also the Strength of Israel will not lie nor repent: for he is
not a man, that he should repent.* —1 Samuel 15:29

This verse seems strange at first, but here, repent
means "to change one's mind," not to ask for forgiveness.
The message is this: God is not fickle. He doesn't waffle
between opinions. When he promises us something, he
will follow through. If he appears to have failed, we must
fix our perception. God sees the spiritual realm more
clearly than we see anything with our eyes. He sees
everything—past, present, future—now that's a reliable
perspective! We find a secure place to stand when we rely
on God and trust him with our whole hearts.

April 29

For the word of God is quick, and powerful, and sharper than any two edged sword, piercing even to the dividing asunder of soul and spirit, and of the joints and marrow, and is a discerner of the thoughts and intents of the heart.

—Hebrews 4:12

This morning I made coffee, checked my phone, signed a permission slip, opened a novel. I dropped the kids at school, checked Facebook, skimmed the news, and answered emails—all this before starting my work day. My mind churned as I envisioned schemes, schedules, emails I might write, ways to exert control. Is it any surprise that with the morning not even behind me, I felt anxious and scattered? Lord, my life is filled with so much information to sense and absorb. Please help me to quiet my mind so that I may receive you; your word pierces the distractions to challenge and bolster my heart.

April 30

∞

And [Solomon] said, Lord God of Israel, there is no God like thee, in heaven above, or on earth beneath, who keepest covenant and mercy with thy servants that walk before thee with all their heart. —**1 Kings 8:23**

Turning our hearts fully toward God is the key to enjoying the fullness of all God promises to those who belong to him. God can't be manipulated. He's not interested in a transactional relationship with us, where he's a means to our ends. God is personal. He's looking for an ongoing conversation with us—one that fills our thoughts and permeates our considerations and influences our decisions. Our relationship with God will always be about truth and love.

May

May 1

But without faith it is impossible to please Him: for he that cometh to God must believe that He is, and that He is a rewarder of them that diligently seek Him. —Hebrews 11:6

Lord, my dear and fine-minded friend is an atheist. He was in the military and has seen unspeakable things; he believes a caring God could not permit such evil. He and I have some good conversations, and most days we come to the conclusion that we must agree to disagree. But sometimes I talk to my friend, or I listen to the news, and despite my best efforts I am filled with fear and uncertainty. God, there are so many doubters in this world—people who question your existence and power. Please fill my heart with belief in you.

May 2

∞

Blessed be the Lord, that hath given rest unto his people Israel, according to all that he promised: there hath not failed one word of all his good promise. —**1 Kings 8:56**

Every day we read about the public failures of actors, athletes, and leaders. We each excel in some areas while failing, sometimes miserably, in others. But there's one exception to this rule of fallibility: God. Centuries before Christ came to earth, God promised it would happen. Today we hold on to the long-ago promise of Christ's return. Do we think God has failed? Or, do we believe, as Paul wrote to the Thessalonians, that God is delaying because he is being patient with us, allowing us the time to turn to him? God always keeps his promises.

May 3

And let us consider one another to provoke unto love and to good works. —**Hebrews 10:24**

I felt cheerful today. The sun was out when I rode to the farmer's market, and I bought a bouquet of flowers to brighten my table. When I met a friend for lunch, I was at my best: joking and affectionate, a good listener. Later that day she emailed to say she'd been in a terrible mood before we met, but our lunch cheered her and inspired her to help a colleague with a tough assignment. I was reminded that what we put into the world has repercussions beyond what we can imagine. Dear God, whom may I inspire to do good today?

May 4

The hand of our God is upon all them for good that seek him.

—Ezra 8:22

Have you ever had someone who is fully "in your corner," someone who has your back at all times, tells you the truth even if it hurts, knows how to encourage you in meaningful ways, and takes the time to invest in your development and growth as a person? If you have, you're blessed—and God promises to be in the corner of those who seek him, who lean in and pursue a relationship with him.

May 5

Therefore we ought to give the more earnest heed to the things which we have heard, lest at any time we should let them slip.

Hebrews 2:1

God, yesterday I visited a painter friend. Watching her add a line of blue to her painting of a copse of trees, I asked, "When do you know when you're done?" She laughed: "Oh, well, I'm never done! I'm always working and growing." She gestured at the painting. "There is always something more to be learned." Following you requires constant study and attention to your word, Lord, lest we lose our way. I am not always as patient as I could be. I am not always as clear-sighted or kind. Teach me to always be attentive to your teachings through worship and the way I interact with others. May I not become complacent in my lifelong faith.

May 6

Blessed are all they that put their trust in him. —**Psalm 2:12**

$\mathcal{P}$salm 2 reminds us of the beatitudes in Matthew 5 where Christ tells his disciples that the meek will one day inherit the earth. God has a plan. Those who are wise and put their trust in God and live humbly before him will find themselves exalted to places of honor, while those who grabbed honor for themselves and trampled others underfoot will face the verdict of the true king, God's Son. Justice will prevail. In the meantime, let's place our trust in the son and wait patiently for him.

May 7

Hatred stirreth up strifes: but love covereth all sins.

– Proverbs 10:12

ℬless this gathering of what, at first glance, looks like mismatched parts, encircling God, for we want to become a family. Guide us as we step closer to one another, but not so close as to crowd. Heal wounds from past events that made this union possible. Bless the children with the courage to try new relatives, new traditions, new homes. Step closer, loving God, and lead us.

May 8

Hereby perceive we the love of God, because he laid down his life for us: and we ought to lay down our lives for the brethren.

—1 John 3:16

We come today, O God, as near strangers gathered from scattered lives, for families no longer live close by. Be the common thread running through our reunion as we recall and rededicate our ancestors' memory. Bless us, Lord of history, the next generation. Bless and guide the young ones, our descendants. As we catch up with each other, embrace us and send us back to our distant homes renewed, refreshed, and revitalized until we once again join hands with you around the family table.

May 9

Herein is my Father glorified, that ye bear much fruit; so shall ye be my disciples. — John 15:8

The surge of adrenaline as we look over our shoulders to see who's gaining on us is as natural as breathing, Lord, and we pick up the pace to keep ahead. Competition is exhilarating, and we welcome its challenges. Yet, competition out of control creates bare-knuckle conflict within us, and we are shocked at the lengths to which we will go to win. We must look ahead to you, not backward to those we're "besting."

May 10

I exhort therefore, that, first of all, supplications, prayers, intercessions, and giving of thanks, be made for all men; For kings, and for all that are in authority; that we may lead a quiet and peaceable life in all godliness and honesty.

—1 Timothy 2:1–2

Life is full of trade-offs, Lord, and I need to make one. Guide my search for a career where I can have both a life and a living. Your balance is not found running in a circle, but along a beckoning path where enough is more than sufficient; where money comes second to family, community, and self; where success takes on new meaning; and where, in the giving up, I gain wealth beyond belief.

May 11

Bless the Lord, ye his angels, that excel in strength, that do his commandments, hearkening unto the voice of his word.

—Psalm 103:20

Dear Lord, sometimes our coworkers feel like family and we are grateful to belong. We do our finest work under the boosted morale of a warm and creative workgroup. Bless the folks down the hall, across the room, in the next department, or in the office next door. They are more than coworkers, they are workday neighbors.

May 12

∞

The heavens declare the glory of God; and the firmament sheweth his handywork. Day unto day uttereth speech, and night unto night sheweth knowledge. There is no speech nor language, where their voice is not heard. Their line is gone out through all the earth, and their words to the end of the world.

—Psalm 19:1–4

May you be the leader you were meant to be today. May you find courage to temper your business goals with an eye toward human compassion. May you carefully weigh the consequences of every tough decision you make—the impact on those around you. May you know that one greater than you goes before you and stands behind you, offering great wisdom.

May 13

∞

Wherefore I put thee in remembrance that thou stir up the gift
of God, which is in thee by the putting on of my hands. For
God hath not given us the spirit of fear; but of power, and of
love, and of a sound mind. – 2 Timothy 1:6–7

Exercise is so good. I lace up my shoes and feel my
engaging muscles sing your praises —you made this warm
machine that I must mindfully care for. I will pray now,
with energy, exertion, gutting it out. But I will not pray
with words for a while. You are here as I pick up speed.
And what, after all, needs to be said aloud at this moment?
How better to honor you than to use the incredible tools
you've given us?

May 14

He staggered not at the promise of God through unbelief; but was strong in faith, giving glory to God; And being fully persuaded that, what he had promised, he was able also to perform. —**Romans 4:20–21**

We are far too easily pleased, Lord. We run after our toys with such vigor. We work and work, earning more and more money, thinking that somehow happiness can be bought, or that the joy of the future can be mortgaged today. But your promise is not found on the "fast track." We must open our hearts and give ourselves over to your word. Give us that vision, God, and the determination to reach for your promises every day.

May 15

Blessed be God, which hath not turned away my prayer, nor his mercy from me. - -Psalm 66:20

I've set a single place at the table, O God, and am dining for the first time without my companion, my lost friend. What can we say to bless this lonely meal? What

words can we use to grace this half-portion of life? Be with me as I swallow around lonely tears. Bless my remembering; inspire me to care for myself in honor of all the love that went before. May I live with this loss, always leaning on you for strength, even when I can finally stand alone.

May 16

Take therefore no thought for the morrow: for the morrow shall take thought for the things of itself. Sufficient unto the day is the evil thereof. —**Matthew 6:34**

God, so much of life is fleeting. It seems like we are always saying goodbye to this person or that situation. But there is one thing we can always count on—your love. Like the foundation upon which our lives are built, your love gives us stability, something to hold onto when everything around us is whirling chaos. Like the roof over our heads, your love shelters us from life's worst storms. Thank you, God, for your everlasting love.

May 17

∞

A new commandment I give unto you, That ye love one another; as I have loved you, that ye also love one another. By this shall all men know that ye are my disciples, if ye have love one to another. —**John 13:34–35**

My biggest fear, God, is that in loving people who oppose you, I fail to stand against the injustices they perpetrate. How do I stand for justice and yet still love my

enemies? Does my love cloak their iniquities? I know in my soul that I must love those people, but still, God, I wonder and fear that love is too easy. Strengthen me to love them, and give me wisdom to know how to extend your love without compromising your justice.

May 18

Brethren, I count not myself to have apprehended: but this one thing I do, forgetting those things which are behind, and reaching forth unto those things which are before, I press toward the mark for the prize of the high calling of God in Christ Jesus. —**Philippians 3:13–14**

It can be tempting to write hope off as weak. We often hear expressions like "I hope it doesn't rain," where hope is an idle wish. But hope matters! Hope, love, and faith are closely related. They are the inseparable sister virtues, each one stronger through association with the other two. When used together, these beautiful qualities multiply their power and result in immense strength. We persevere in the Lord with this strength!

May 19

Now the Lord is that Spirit: and where the Spirit of the Lord is, there is liberty. —2 Corinthians 3:17

We have been guilty, Lord, of looking for our leaders in places of wealth and influence. We want to glorify the outwardly successful, passing over those who have learned to live wisely and with integrity. Rather, we tend to follow after those who give blithe answers with the appearance of absolute confidence. But you have offered us better, we know. Your spirit fills those who walk in humility, patience, and self-sacrifice. Please open our eyes that we may see those gentle faces beckoning us upward and onward in a spirit of love.

May 20

Now we exhort you, brethren, warn them that are unruly, comfort the feebleminded, support the weak, be patient toward all men. —1 Thessalonians 5:14

Lord, we need your help to move beyond the times we hurt one another and the times we willingly misunderstand; the times we assume we know all there is to know and turn away. And then there are the times that we make private rules only to publicly condemn anyone who fails to abide by them, limiting one another by labeling, interpreting, conditioning, insisting, resisting, defining. From all this, Lord, we come, asking that you forgive us as we forgive those "others" we need new eyes to see and ears to hear. Be with us as we do so.

May 21

Blessed is the man that trusteth in the Lord, and whose hope the Lord is. —**Jeremiah 17:7**

Living in difficult times requires us to maintain a positive, hopeful attitude about the future. Having hope is vital for our mental, physical, and spiritual health. Lord, help me move into the future with a steadfast spirit, looking forward in faith and hope and trusting in the promises you have made to your people.

May 22

And let us not be weary in well doing: for in due season we shall reap, if we faint not. —**Galatians 6:9**

Bless the soil beneath our feet and the sky overhead, and make us one with it. We are catching on, catching up with ourselves, creator God, and catching a glimpse of the fading streams and trash-strewn seas we have long ignored. Bless and use our reclamation efforts, for it is a task we can't accomplish alone. With your help, we can bind up and reclaim this poor old earth. We feel whispers of hope in the winds of changed hearts and minds. We are grateful for another chance.

May 23

I wait for the Lord, my soul doth wait, and in his word do I hope. —Psalm 130:5

Help me to slow down, God of patience, because sometimes I'm so frustrated by this tough daily grind. I know you have a plan for me and I see your good works in my life and those of my loved ones. But it's hard to keep my mind clear of negative clutter when I'm in my routine, caring for my spouse or children, going to work, feeling stuck. In your word I find moments of peace, the promise of quietude.

May 24

And hope maketh not ashamed; because the love of God is shed abroad in our hearts by the Holy Ghost which is given unto us. —**Romans 5:5**

Lord, the news of the world has made me a cynic. I hear myself giving up and even bonding with my loved ones over how we've *all* given up. We need to stop this idle cynicism and take heart. God, you made us and you made hope for us, and there is no clearer promise than your holy word. May your love take root in our hearts and make us

into better friends, neighbors, and citizens of this vibrant world.

May 25

∞

And Jesus called a little child unto him, and set him in the midst of them, And said, Verily I say unto you, Except ye be converted, and become as little children, ye shall not enter into the kingdom of heaven. Whosoever therefore shall humble himself as this little child, the same is greatest in the kingdom of heaven. —Matthew 18:2–4

Today I kicked off my "grown-up" shoes and played barefoot in the yard. So much of life is complex and demanding but the greatest pleasures and fulfillments can be simple: A warm, sunny day; a sound night's sleep; a child's hand to hold while we watch cartoons together. Lord, your love for me is simple and powerful, and I am humbled by its magnitude.

May 26

The people that walked in darkness have seen a great light: they that dwell in the land of the shadow of death, upon them hath the light shined. —Isaiah 9:2

Television isn't the place to look for sincerity, but I can feel tempted by the ministries of those who claim God smiles on us with earthly wealth. Every day we work hard for what seems like less and less, and I look to you, Lord, for answers why I'm not more successful, why my family struggles, why so many others have so much more. Please

help me to remember that money may be here and now but your kingdom is forever and ever.

May 27

∞

For whosoever will save his life shall lose it; but whosoever shall lose his life for my sake and the gospel's, the same shall save it. For what shall it profit a man, if he shall gain the whole world, and lose his own soul? —Mark 8:35-36

We've all heard stories of wealthy people who left their riches to charity, surprising everyone. Often the real story is how their children try to overturn these wills, claiming that only a person not in his right mind could give away so much. But Mark tells us plainly that it is only those in their right minds who give it all away. To gently tread in the footsteps of Christ we must leave our heaviest possessions and be ready to carry others who may not know the way.

May 28

But love ye your enemies, and do good, and lend, hoping for nothing again; and your reward shall be great, and ye shall be the children of the Highest: for he is kind unto the unthankful and to the evil. Be ye therefore merciful, as your Father also is merciful. —**Luke 6:35-36**

Today someone almost ran me over as I crossed the street—he was talking on the phone and didn't look where he was turning. It is the single biggest challenge of my life to forgive and love the ignorant and unrepentant. I feel humiliated and ashamed of how hard it is. But I know I'm not alone, God, because time and again we read in your holy word about forgiveness and mercy. We must hear it over and over to remind ourselves constantly to keep you in our hearts and keep our hearts open.

May 29

Delight thyself also in the Lord: and he shall give thee the desires of thine heart. —**Psalm 37:4**

God, I'm on such a roll. My children are doing well in school and activities; they're getting along with each other and acting like gracious, grown-up people. Maybe I'll change my mind a week from now but these moments are a great triumph. We parents do the hard daily work of teaching our children what's right and wrong, but the lessons all come from you, Lord, our guiding light. Thank you for this glimpse of the wonderful someday-adults we're hoping and working to raise together.

May 30

I will also praise thee with the psaltery, even thy truth, O my God: unto thee will I sing with the harp, O thou Holy One of Israel. —**Psalm 71:22**

When my siblings and I were little, our parents sent us to church camp. We were excited to swim and play ball and share bunkbeds with new friends, and sat through our bible studies with great reluctance and fidgeting. But Lord, I would give anything to feel the same joy I felt as we sang worship songs around the campfire. Something about music speaks to our souls so directly, and I love that you gave the gift of song for us to celebrate and gather together. Thank you for so much beauty and fellowship.

May 31

And this is life eternal, that they might know thee the only true God, and Jesus Christ, whom thou hast sent. —John 17:3

Once I talked with a friend who always said he was a Christian. "Do you believe in Jesus Christ Almighty as your lord and savior?" I said. He said he didn't, but that he'd been raised a Christian and still felt like he was one. But Lord, I know that isn't good enough. You sent your son to earth that we might all be saved from our sins. We must love one another but we must also believe in you and the sacrifice you made, the son you gave, to give us a chance to follow you for eternity. Please help my friend to find you, and help me to keep you in my heart. Amen.

June

June 1

Blessed are the pure in heart: for they shall see God.
—Matthew 5:8

Lord, my youngest daughter is the sweetest person I've ever met. Sometimes I can't believe she belongs to us. She loves every person and thing down to ladybugs and daddy long legs, and she radiates goodness and loving kindness wherever we go. I know that she'll grow up and change at least a little, but these beautiful early years are such a blessing. Please walk with me as I help her to protect her spirit as she learns about the world and finds her place in it. I know she will love you as I do and rely on you for strength and courage to be herself.

June 2

But know that the Lord hath set apart him that is godly for himself: the Lord will hear when I call unto him.

—Psalm 4:3

To feel listened to—to be heard—is one of the best gifts we can receive from another human being, especially when we're hurting or in distress. Often, though, while people who love and care for us can hear us out, they are powerless to change our situation or our inner landscape. God, who invites those who walk in his ways to call on him, not only listens to our petitions and pleas but also intervenes on our behalf. He will hear every call for help and respond, providing his all-surpassing peace to keep hearts and minds in Christ Jesus. Are you troubled about something today? Call on him—he is listening!

June 3

For the righteous Lord loveth righteousness; his countenance
doth behold the upright.

—Psalm 11:7

There are so many expressions of God's love
throughout his Word! If we were to count them all, we'd
find hundreds of "love notes" sprinkled throughout the
scriptures. And when we regularly take time to read and
meditate on these expressions of God's loving-kindness,
absorbing their truth, we grow increasingly secure in
him. Eventually, we are hardly disturbed by those who
would try to make
us feel rejected or
unworthy of love.

June 4

∞

I will instruct thee and teach thee in the way which thou shalt go: I will guide thee with mine eye.

—Psalm 32:8

Most of us wouldn't head out on Class 3 river rapids without a guide, nor would we venture out in an unfamiliar city after dark without someone beside us who knew where it was safe to go and where it wasn't. Fortunately, God is a gracious guide and will patiently get us back on track as we yield control to him. To entrust ourselves to his wisdom and love is to be certain of ultimately landing in our desired haven, to be brought safely home to spend eternity beside him when our journey on earth is complete.

June 5

∞

For as the heaven is high above the earth, so great is his mercy toward them that fear him. As far as the east is from the west, so far hath he removed our transgressions from us.

—Psalm 103:11-12

One of the most debilitating emotions we can experience is shame. Maybe as a child you used to hear the rebuke, "Shame on you!" We can carry the impact of shaming for years; its shadow can darken our hearts and our days. From our past experiences, we may even have come to believe that God is in the business of shaming, that he wants us to know how shameful we are. How untrue! Read the verses on this page again, slowly. Absorb the words. Replace "his" and "he" with "God's" and "God." God is for you. God forgives all of it. Starting today, let him wash away any shame you've been carrying. It's time to be free.

June 6

∞

The Lord shall preserve thy going out and thy coming in from this time forth, and even for evermore.

—Psalm 121:8

Some of us carry pepper spray, some of us have a big dog, some of us have taken self-defense classes. Do you employ any particular safety measures? There's nothing wrong with being prepared, but ultimately we are not in control of everything that happens to us—no matter who we are. So here we are, vulnerable people in an often-dangerous world. How do we keep from worrying about worst-case scenarios? Only by remembering Psalm 121. God's watch over our lives is continual. We can call out to him for help at all times. So even as you do your best to be safe today, be at peace. God is watching over you.

June 7

*Though a sinner do evil an hundred times, and his days be
prolonged, yet surely I know that it shall be well with them
that fear God, which fear before him.*

—Psalm 9:1

The Bible's writers vent their frustration from time
to time when it seems the bad guys aren't getting their
comeuppance. And the writers seem to hear it, too,
because they eventually land in the right place. What is
that place? It's the place of trusting God's timing, trusting
his plan for justice. He does have a plan, and he will carry
it out. Those who make it their aim to honor God will not
be overlooked but are seen, known, and blessed by God.

June 8

Come now, and let us reason together, saith the Lord: though your sins be as scarlet, they shall be as white as snow; though they be red like crimson, they shall be as wool.

—Isaiah 1:18

As humans, we seem to have a knack for entertaining wrong notions about God's character. For example, sometimes we view God as unreasonable and unpleasable. This harmful belief is often followed by an even more harmful conclusion: that it's pointless to try having a relationship with him. And yet here in Isaiah, God speaks words that reveal that he is anything but unreasonable and unpleasable.

June 9

∞

Therefore the Lord himself shall give you a sign; Behold, a virgin shall conceive, and bear a son, and shall call his name Immanuel.

—Isaiah 7:14

This verse is a near-far promise. What does that mean? It means it is a promise that had a immediate fulfillment as well as a future one. The second fulfillment—the far-off one—is the one we're most familiar with, and for good reason. But this promise also foretells one of the most important signs of Jesus' birth, as Mary, not yet having known a man, would conceive not by physical means but by the intervention of God.

June 10

Fear thou not; for I am with thee: be not dismayed; for I am thy God: I will strengthen thee; yea, I will help thee; yea, I will uphold thee with the right hand of my righteousness.

—Isaiah 41:10

There are around 100 "fear nots" in the Bible, which can certainly be called a biblical theme. And these assurances are more than enough to remind us to leave fear behind and keep our focus on God's rock-solid promises that remind us of his sufficiency, strength, and steadfastness. Although people may fail us, God is fully trustworthy, and with him by ourside, come what may, we need never fear.

June 11

Thus saith the Lord, thy Redeemer, the holy One of Israel;
I am the Lord thy God . . . which leadeth thee by the way
that thou shouldest go.

—Isaiah 48:17

In this age of GPS technology, navigation has become a snap. But even GPS devices have their limitations, and folks have been steered wrong by them. Have you had that happen? That's when it's time to pull off the road and consult someone who knows. That's when it's time to stop and take time to pray, seeking God's direction to get us back on track. He promises he will lead us in the way we need to go, if only we will let him.

June 12

For, behold, I create new heavens and a new earth: and the former shall not be remembered, nor come into mind.

—Isaiah 65:17

This world has had some troubled chapters—our personal lives have them as well. We suffer, we mourn, we recover, we find peace and even some joy along our way. But God's ultimate plan does not leave things this way. In the Old and New testaments, God's word describes his plan for a new heavens and a new earth—an "ever after" that is real and much more than merely happy. Tears and pain will be a thing of the distant past. The memory of them will leave us.

June 13

∞

This I recall to my mind, therefore have I hope. It is of the Lord's mercies that we are not consumed, because his compassions fail not. They are new every morning: great is thy faithfulness.
—Lamentations 3:21-23

Many hymnals that were the staple of church music only a generation ago included the perennial favorite "Great Is Thy Faithfulness." With a beautiful melody and timeless message, it continues to be sung today, even in more contemporary worship sets. The hymn's author wrote of God's faithfulness manifested through his changeless character, his amazing creation, and his provisions of redemption, peace, and blessing in our lives. The refrain ends with a heart cry of gratitude: "Great is Thy faithfulness, Lord, unto me!"

June 14

∞

And it shall come to pass . . . that I will pour out my spirit upon all flesh.

—Joel 2:28

After Jesus' ascension, his disciples did as he had instructed and waited prayerfully for the promise. At Pentecost, ten days after Jesus had left them (promising he would return one day), the Spirit was poured out in an unmistakable way. The promise of God's presence with us by his Spirit is a gift that remains with us today. All who belong to Christ have the identifying mark or seal of God's Spirit working in their lives and are called to daily follow his direction and leading.

June 15

∞

But thou, Bethlehem Ephratah, though thou be little among the thousands of Judah, yet out of thee shall he come forth unto me that is to be ruler in Israel; whose goings forth have been from of old, from everlasting.

–Micah 5:2

Bethlehem is a small town, the place King David was from. It was the place from which God promised, through his servant Micah, that a ruler from eternity would one day emerge. Jesus, the promised Messiah, was born there some 700 years after Micah's prophecy. Jesus used metaphors to help people understand the spiritual significance of who he was and what he had come to do. In one of these explanations, he referred to himself as the Bread of Life—certainly it's no coincidence that Bethlehem itself means "House of Bread."

June 16

But unto you that fear my name shall the Sun of righteousness arise with healing in his wings; and ye shall go forth, and grow up as calves of the stall.

—Malachi 4:2

The imagery of Malachi 4:2 is of calves leaping and frolicking after being let loose to pasture. Have you ever stopped to watch as calves or little lambs leap and kick because they feel excited to be alive? It's an image that goes beyond mere peace and contentment, to a state of unbridled joy and elation. It's something God wants us to know he has planned for those who love him and walk in his ways.

June 17

∞

But as many as received him, to them gave he power to become the sons of God, even to them that believe on his name.

—John 1:12

Anyone who has ever navigated an adoption process knows how difficult it can be— how detailed the paperwork and drawn-out the waiting. God has gone through an adoption process—a very costly one—to open the path for us to join his family. All that is left to be done now is for us to receive the welcome into his home by believing on his son's name —entrusting ourselves to him and to what he has done to save us.

June 18

$$\infty$$

Verily, verily, I say unto you, he that heareth my word, and believeth on him that sent me, hath everlasting life, and shall not come into condemnation; but is passed from death unto life.

—John 5:24

When we think about threats to our lives, we generally think of such things as sickness, disease, and accidents. But Jesus had another much more serious problem in mind when he came to earth to rescue us from death. Whether we realize it or not, the real danger we are facing is related to our sin and the condemnation brings when we stand before God. And that's just what Jesus came to address—our sin predicament. He paid the price for our sin with his own life and opened the way for us to be made right with God.

June 19

For I am not ashamed of the gospel of Christ: for it is the power of God unto salvation to every one that believeth.

—Romans 1:16

Sometimes we're afraid the gospel won't do its job, so we try to help it along with glitzy church events. Or we leave out the uncomfortable parts to talk about, like where it says all of us have fallen short of what it takes to make it to heaven. Yet here in Romans 1:16, God promises that the gospel itself is God's powerful means of salvation. Just telling it like it is: We're sinners who need a savior, and Jesus is that savior; when we entrust ourselves to him and receive his word and works, we are given the gift of eternal life.

June 20

∞

And we know that all things work together for good to them that love God, to them who are the called according to his purpose.

—Romans 8:28

This verse is often quoted only up to the word "good," which allows for a misrepresentation of its message. It's a promise not for everyone in general, but for those who entrust themselves to God and who walk in a loving relationship with him. We'll see God faithfully bringing about spiritual growth and spiritual blessings through our experiences and trials as we make our way through life.

June 21

∞

Now thanks be unto God, which always causeth us to triumph in Christ, and maketh manifest the savour of his knowledge by us in every place.

—2 Corinthians 2:14

Have you ever known someone whose perfume or cologne is so distinctive that you could know they're there without seeing them? This verse is talking about the spiritual "fragrance" that marks those who are in Christ. Sometimes we just know when someone else is a believer; they have that bearing, that different countenance. They're peaceful, gentle, genuine. That's God's presence in them, making himself known. It's the promise of the triumph of Christ in their lives in a tangible expression we can sense.

June 22

And God is able to make all grace abound toward you; that ye, always having all sufficiency in all things, may abound to every good work.

—2 Corinthians 9:8

Sometimes when a person is considering the repercussions of surrendering their life to Christ, they think (and sometimes say), I could never possibly get past these things and live up to those standards. We can tell them, "You're absolutely right! You never could follow Christ if it were up to you and your own resources to do it. But I've got some good news for you. . . ." God never expects nor requires us to walk in our own strength. That's why he has given us his Spirit, and that's why he pours out his grace in our lives to enable us to "abound in every good work."

June 23

∞

Blessed be the God and Father of our Lord Jesus Christ, who hath blessed us with all spiritual blessings in heavenly places in Christ.

—Ephesians 1:3

Some folks would have us believe that God is something like a cosmic vending machine. If we present the right kind of coin (faith), we can elicit from God whatever gift we choose. By contrast, however, the blessings God has in mind for us are far better than anything in this world, better than our physical life, even. God's blessings are sacred, priceless gifts given to us from his personal spiritual treasury.

June 24

For we are his workmanship, created in Christ Jesus unto good works, which God hath before ordained that we should walk in them.

—Ephesians 2:10

God is operating in our lives like a master craftsman, working to form in us the kind of life we long for as ones who want to please him. Those who love God long to one day present to him a life well-spent, doing what honors and glorifies him. But he knows us so well that he already prepared what he knew we'd want and need in advance.

June 25

∞

I know whom I have believed, and am persuaded that he is able to keep that which I have committed unto him against that day.

—2 Timothy 1:12

Nothing we do in service to Christ will be lost or overlooked. Everything we offer to him, everything we do to honor him, no matter how hidden from onlookers, will be remembered and rewarded on the day we are to present ourselves before Christ. Are you doing good that is being overlooked? God sees. God knows. Entrust it all to his care.

June 26

All scripture is given by inspiration of God, and is profitable for doctrine, for reproof, for correction, for instruction in righteousness: That the man of God may be perfect, thoroughly furnished unto all good works.

—2 Timothy 3:16-17

"If God would write a note on a rock and throw it through my window!" a young woman lamented. She wanted an answer from God to a difficult situation. The reality we often overlook in our life struggles is that the Bible is God's personal message to us. Its message is "living and active"—relevant and pertinent to each person's life, God speaking by his Spirit through the pages as we read them.

June 27

∞

Henceforth there is laid up for me a crown of righteousness, which the Lord, the righteous judge, shall give me at that day: and not to me only, but unto all them also that love his appearing.

2 Timothy 4:8

As the apostle Paul reached the end of his earthly journey, he reflected on what was ahead. Paul knew that because he fully entrusted himself to Christ, he would be received into heaven and his faith would be rewarded. Paul says clearly in this verse that this is the promise that all believers in Christ can count on. The crown of righteousness Paul mentions may or may not be literal, but it will certainly be our crowning moment when we are made complete in Christ, righteous and free from the reach of sin and death.

June 28

And the Lord shall deliver me from every evil work, and will preserve me unto his heavenly kingdom: to whom be glory for ever and ever. Amen.

—2 Timothy 4:18

Paul's confident assertions are not merely wishful thinking or "the power of positive thinking." They are based in his knowledge of and trust in God's promises. Paul knew the Old Testament scriptures inside and out; he never doubted God's word. How about us? Do we pray this confidently in God's promises? Do we know the assurances we have from God? As we spend time in God's Word, we will grow increasingly familiar with what he has told us and what we can be sure of.

June 29

Knowing this, that the trying of your faith worketh patience. But let patience have her perfect work, that ye may be perfect and entire, wanting nothing.

—Psalm 9:1

One of the hardest things for us to do is to wait patiently--whether it's waiting in rush-hour traffic, waiting for some important test results, or waiting for the delayed flight to arrive home with our loved one. And yet the scriptures are full of commands for us to wait for God's timing, part of the faith- and patience-growing process. Will we trust, no matter how long we've waited, that what our heavenly Father determines is best? When we are able to wait patiently with our hands and hearts open to God in this way, our faith is complete, lacking nothing.

June 30

But whoso looketh into the perfect law of liberty, and continueth therein, he being not a forgetful hearer, but a doer of the work, this man shall be blessed in his deed.

—James 1:25

Obedience and faith are synonymous concepts in the Bible. James, the brother of Jesus, wrote to oppose the false notion that as long as we professed faith in Christ, it didn't matter how we lived. Rather, a true believer is one whose life reflects the reality of their faith. Of course, James was not saying that our good works are what save us. That would be getting the cart before the horse. We are saved by grace through faith in Christ alone. But the hallmark of a truly faith-filled person is that the old way of living falls away as we strive to become more and more like Christ. This is the life that God promises to bless.

July

July 1

∞

*Submit yourselves therefore to God. Resist the devil,
and he will flee from you.*

—James 4:7

Sometimes we spend too long wrestling with our temptations. Eventually we are worn down and give in. Why do we do this? Most often it's because, in our heart of hearts, we haven't truly submitted our will to God in the matter. The struggle is not about the power of the temptation or the weakness of our resolve or the need to just be stronger. It's this: we have yet to fully surrender our desires to God. Once we do, we can look to God for the strength to say no; and as we turn our faces fully toward Christ, the tempter will not stand a chance, guaranteed.

July 2

∞

Now when he had left speaking, he said unto Simon, Launch out into the deep, and let down your nets for a draught.

—Luke 5:4

When we believe in each other we act as angels, offering our confidence and the power of our faith. It is no small thing to look into another's eyes, straight and true, and to say with sincerity, "I believe in you." As Simon trusted in the Lord, we use our faith to help one another.

July 3

And righteousness shall be the girdle of his loins, and faithfulness the girdle of his reins.

—Isaiah 11:5

In this day of bigger is best, Lord, we wonder what difference our little lights can make. Remind us of the laser, so tiny, yet when focused, has infinite power. This little light of mine, O Lord, give it such focus.

July 4

I am the Lord, and there is none else, there is no God beside me.

—Isaiah 45:5

I get discouraged, O God, my comforter and guide, and feel overwhelmed, which makes me even more discouraged. The messages are everywhere, from magazine ads defining unattainable standards of beauty to movies that glamorize a certain type of car, or a house of a certain size. Sometimes I fear that I cannot live up to the faith that my children put in me, that I am not as strong or as invincible as they believe me to be. Lead me beyond negative thoughts and useless circles of worry to a renewed frame of mind. Work your miracle of transformation in me.

July 5

A bruised reed shall he not break, and the smoking flax shall he not quench: he shall bring forth judgment unto truth.

—Isaiah 42:3

Nothing about God's children is too trivial or ordinary, too overwhelming or dreadful to be overlooked. God's ear is as close as a bent knee, a bowed head, or clasped hands. We simply need to plug ourselves into God's nurturing care.

July 6

Into thine hand I commit my spirit: thou hast redeemed me,
O Lord God of truth.

—Psalm 31:5

Sometimes, God, I get too persnickety and alarmingly tidy. I suppose I think it's a way I can control my life. When that happens, shake me up like a snow globe so I can be real. Truly, messily, and welcomingly real.

July 7

∞

*But the heavens and the earth, which are now, by the same
word are kept in store, reserved unto fire against the day of
judgment and perdition of ungodly men.*

—2 Peter 3:8

When trouble strikes, O God, we are
restored by small signs of hope found in ordinary
places: friends, random kindness, shared pain
and support. Help us collect them like mustard
seeds that can grow into a spreading harvest.

July 8

I have not hid thy righteousness within my heart; I have declared thy faithfulness and thy salvation: I have not concealed thy lovingkindness and thy truth from the great congregation.

—Psalm 40:10

Thank you for always being there to hold my hand when I am scared, cheer me up when I am sad, and keep me company when I am alone. You are the one constant in my life, my true North Star.

July 9

It is better to hear the rebuke of the wise, than for a man to hear the song of fools.

—Ecclesiastes 7:5

When we love our friends, we see their goodness and beauty, no matter what they look like, how old they are, what they choose to wear. When we learn to recognize the soul underneath these outward trappings, the faith and life's works, our own lives are enriched.

July 10

If any man speak, let him speak as the oracles of God; if any man minister, let him do it as of the ability which God giveth: that God in all things may be glorified through Jesus Christ, to whom be praise and dominion for ever and ever. Amen.

1 Peter 4:11

What would it be like to soar in Heaven? What would it be like to worship as naturally as you breathe? What would it be like to dance in the light of God? Hold that thought as long as you can.

July 11

O Lord God of hosts, who is a strong Lord like unto thee?
or to thy faithfulness round about thee?

—Psalm 89:8

God wants us to know peace is in every area of our lives—peace in our daily work, our business, our family, our soul. The key to letting peace enter in is to invite God into each of these areas daily. When we walk among the faithful, we surround ourselves with your might.

July 12

∞

But the Lord said unto Samuel, Look not on his countenance, or on the height of his stature; because I have refused him: for the Lord seeth not as man seeth; for man looketh on the outward appearance, but the Lord looketh on the heart.

—1 Samuel 16:7

When teetering here on the "cutting edge" of technology, cyberspace, and everything in between, O God, it is reassuring to know that from the beginning of time, you guide, direct, and hear our voices as we continue to ask for guidance. Our scenery changes but you are eternal.

July 13

Commit thy way unto the Lord; trust also in him;
and he shall bring it to pass.

—Psalm 37:5

I value the well-worn paths of our years together in faith, Lord, those lined with thorns as well as roses, those rutted with roughness as much as those with smooth, rounded joys. My loved ones fill my days with the ups and downs of earthly life, but you are my strength.

July 14

*Mine enemies would daily swallow me up: for they be many
that fight against me, O thou most High. What time I am
afraid, I will trust in thee. In God I will praise his word, in God
I have put my trust; I will not fear what flesh can do unto me.*

—Psalm 56:2–4

First we are hurt, and feelings of anger may
consume us. Then thoughts of how we can get
revenge come creeping in. But only when we are
ready to relinquish the hurt is there an opportunity
for forgiveness and healing to begin.

July 15

The living, the living, he shall praise thee, as I do this day: the father to the children shall make known thy truth.

—Isaiah 38:19

My siblings and I were competitors during our childhood. After all, we had to share a lot—a bedroom, clothes, our parents' attentions. Years later, we're vying for something we never shared before—understanding and affection—the blessings of life as adults with our own families.

July 16

Turn away mine eyes from beholding vanity;
and quicken thou me in thy way.

—Psalm 119:37

When things go wrong, God is usually the first we blame. Forgive us for even considering that you would deliberately hurt one of your very own children. For what could you possibly have to gain? Thank you for your presence; forgive our hubris and easy blame of you.

July 17

He that oppresseth the poor reproacheth his Maker: but he that honoureth him hath mercy on the poor.

—Proverbs 14:31

Help me be creative, O God, as I find heroes for my children, looking past comic book characters and media royalty to those who make a difference in their lives. It can be an exciting scavenger hunt, for there is much good. Lord, guide me toward those deserving role models.

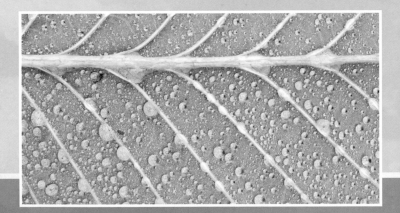

July 18

*And they departed quickly from the sepulchre with fear and
great joy; and did run to bring his disciples word.*

—Matthew 28:8

To find love, we think we must first find the courage
to take a big chance by risking our heart to another; yet it's
only then that we discover
it's in the very act of
offering ourselves that
love is found. So it goes
with God: when we offer
ourselves we find
the fear and great joy.

July 19

Teach me to do thy will; for thou art my God: thy spirit is good; lead me into the land of uprightness.

—Psalm 143:10

To love means always to act with kindness and in the best interests of the other person. God's love lifts us from our low times, but it is not easy. We may have to do things that will hurt one another, but only out of necessity, and only with the greatest honesty and compassion.

July 20

Wherefore seeing we also are compassed about with so great a cloud of witnesses, let us lay aside every weight, and the sin which doth so easily beset us, and let us run with patience the race that is set before us.

—Hebrews 12:1

Sitting in a waiting room, O God, time drags and fear festers. Remake worry into energized, active prayers, into trust in the process of healing and recovery. We're scooting over to make room for you, a companion for the waiting.

July 21

Who is wise, and he shall understand these things? prudent, and he shall know them? for the ways of the Lord are right, and the just shall walk in them: but the transgressors shall fall therein.

—Hosea 14:9

A good day's work, the sweat of your brow, the challenge of the task, a job well done. Even angels may not know the joy a person knows of simply going at the task at hand and finishing it with satisfaction. Thank you, God, for this special feeling.

July 22

If ye abide in me, and my words abide in you, ye shall ask what ye will, and it shall be done unto you.

—John 15:7

God gave me two shoulders to carry my burdens, a creative mind to figure out solutions, and a strong heart to weather disappointments. He gave his own son so that I might find salvation. I rely on my family and my support system for earthly guidance, but we all understand that the true way can only be lighted by the Lord.

July 23

∞

God is a Spirit: and they that worship him must worship him in spirit and in truth.

—John 4:24

For millennia we have painted likenesses of God on walls, ceilings, and canvases. For years we have tried to capture his "personal" likeness. We must not forget to put as much effort into understanding and recognizing the spiritual meaning of our Lord as we have put into how we visualize him. His power and his glory are the world's greatest mystery, a gift that only we can decide to allow into our lives.

July 24

Thine, O Lord is the greatness, and the power, and the glory,
and the victory, and the majesty: for all that is in the heaven
and in the earth is thine; thine is the kingdom, O Lord,
and thou art exalted as head above all.

—1 Chronicles 29:11

Faith cannot be seen or touched or put in a box
or marked on a map. It is not an object or a thing but
a way of moving through the world unrestrained by
the limitations, beliefs, or desires of others. Faith
imbues us with the unseen power of the Lord and
offers our earthly lives to his will.

July 25

For as many as are led by the Spirit of God,
they are the sons of God.

—Romans 8:14

Encourage your child to learn, to master, to question—
to try. It may feel like a big adventure and maybe even a
huge risk, but you can relax, knowing that God is blessing
the undertaking and providing the fuel for the journey.
Many of us lose our will to try as we get older and feel that
our time and options are limited, but the path of God
urges constant reflection and growth.

July 26

For our light affliction, which is but for a moment, worketh for us a far more exceeding and eternal weight of glory; While we look not at the things which are seen, but at the things which are not seen: for the things which are seen are temporal; but the things which are not seen are eternal.

—2 Corinthians 4:17–18

At times we are blinded by our sorrow, Lord. Lift our eyes and bless us, O Father, with a defiant hope, steadfast trust, and fire in the belly to emerge from this trial victorious and whole once again, standing in the light you've given us. Let our faith guide us out of the darkness.

July 27

Continue in prayer, and watch in the same with thanksgiving.
—Colossians 4:2

If we look hard enough, we find blessings in everything—even dirty dishes, unwashed laundry, and chocolate stains on the kitchen floor. Those things remind us that we are part of a family, and in our gratitude and thanksgiving we are part of God's family. Lord, give us watchful eyes to notice your love in the beautiful family chaos that surrounds us.

July 28

∞

The thief cometh not, but for to steal, and to kill, and to destroy: I am come that they might have life, and that they might have it more abundantly.

—John 10:10

Thieves operate on a premise of self preservation. They'll do whatever they have to do to escape being caught. Your life is of no consequence to them. This is a picture of the devil's disposition toward us—like a thief who has come to steal, kill, and destroy. Dark stuff! In absolute contrast to this is Christ's sacrificial love for us. He is so invested in meeting our need for redemption, so concerned about our eternal destiny, that he has come down to us from heaven to take care of the matter.

July 29

Jesus said unto her, I am the resurrection, and the life:
he that believeth in me, though he were dead, yet shall he live:
And whosoever liveth and believeth in me shall never die.
Believest thou this?

—John 11:25-26

Jesus spoke these words to Martha, the sister of Lazarus, after her brother had died. Jesus asked her point blank if she trusted that he held the authority over death that belongs only to God. What a powerful moment! Her brother was dead. He had been in the grave four days—the point of no return in that climate. How does one answer Jesus when he is calling us to trust him against all odds? Then Jesus called Lazarus out of his tomb.

July 30

Therefore if any man be in Christ, he is a new creature: old things are passed away; behold, all things are become new.

—2 Corinthians 5:17

Guide me, O God, as I encourage my loved ones to be positive—to see the good in each day, each person, each challenge. Let them use faith to bolster themselves in a world that can seem random at best. Hope and optimism are gifts from your hand that can guide them for life.

July 31

∞

And in the morning, rising up a great while before day, he went out, and departed into a solitary place, and there prayed.

—Mark 1:35

Through time and trial, we are burnished and polished, our rough edges are smoothed, and we're made more interesting with the nicks and bumps that come with a life well lived. The hard work of nurturing our families and our faith makes us tenacious and durable. Each of our seeming imperfections only makes us more beautiful.

August

August 1

For who is God, save the Lord? and who is a rock, save our God? God is my strength and power: and he maketh my way perfect. He maketh my feet like hinds' feet: and setteth me upon my high places.

—2 Samuel 22:32–34

It's impossible to thank God completely for all that he's taught us. But then again, the best lesson he's shared is that nothing is impossible. Thank you, Lord, for your dazzling arsenal of gifts. Thank you for extending the horizons of my world as I revel in your word.

August 2

Except the Lord build the house, they labour in vain that build it: except the Lord keep the city, the watchman waketh but in vain. It is vain for you to rise up early, to sit up late, to eat the bread of sorrows: for so he giveth his beloved sleep.

—Psalm 127:1–2

O God, when I'm tempted to answer questions my children haven't even asked or give simple answers when they need to discover something on their own, gently shush my mouth and still my thoughts. I am to guide, not to do everything.

August 3

*For I am the Lord your God: ye shall therefore sanctify
yourselves, and ye shall be holy.*

—Leviticus 11:44

Tragedy often serves as a wake-up call, urging
strangers to step away from themselves and move
toward others. We thank God in good times but must
also thank him when life has thrown us and given us
extreme challenges. Neighbors who never knew each
other suddenly realize the world is much friendlier
when they reach out in fellowship.

August 4

*For I know that my redeemer liveth, and that he shall stand at
the latter day upon the earth: And though after my skin
worms destroy this body, yet in my flesh shall I see God.*

—Job 19:25–26

Wise is the soul that cherishes the present without
longing for other times. Fortunate is the heart that loves
without yearning for what it
once had. And blessed is the
mind that is at peace with
today, with eyes and mind
on the promise of eternal
life at the hand of the Lord.

August 5

And he said, The things which are impossible with men are possible with God.

—Luke 18:27

When we are missing an important ingredient in the recipe, we sometimes replace an essential ingredient with something that will do in a pinch. Remind us, O Lord, that when it comes to nourishing our faith, there is no substitute for genuine sharing and caring. We cannot substitute for the hard work of learning and living your word.

August 6

And whatsoever ye do in word or deed, do all in the name of the Lord Jesus, giving thanks to God and the Father by him.

—Colossians 3:17

Bless these children, God. They are beautiful and strong, growing in faith and spirit, in mind and body. Keep them ever moving and reaching out toward the objects of their curiosity. And may they find, in all their explorations, the one thing that holds it all together: your love.

August 7

And be not conformed to this world: but be ye transformed by the renewing of your mind, that ye may prove what is that good, and acceptable, and perfect, will of God.

—Romans 12:2

Recognizing the presence of God around you may make you feel like you've walked from the shadows into the warmth of sunshine. Suddenly, you feel the nourishment that comes from someone taking the time to look out for you and, as it sometimes seems, you alone.

August 8

*But grow in grace, and in the knowledge of our Lord and Saviour
Jesus Christ. To him be glory both now and for ever. Amen.*

—2 Peter 3:18

Children ask the most amazing questions, wise God.
"Grown-ups" are supposed to have all the answers; help
me live with my ignorance. Remind me that I don't need
all the answers, just a willingness to consider the
questions and honor the questioners.

August 9

Humble yourselves in the sight of the Lord,
and he shall lift you up.

—James 4:10

God offers a voice of reason as well as a voice of inspiration. When things are going well, he can remind us to keep our feet on the ground. When things are tough, he can remind us to aim for the stars.

August 10

And he changeth the times and the seasons: he removeth kings, and setteth up kings: he giveth wisdom unto the wise, and knowledge to them that know understanding

—Daniel 2:21

We respond to stresses in our lives with either fear or faith. Fear is a great threat to our faith. That's why we read often in the scriptures the directive to "Fear not." The closer we draw to God, the more our fears diminish. As we witness his awesome power, we are able to trust more in his will.

August 11

Yea, though I walk through the valley of the shadow of death,
I will fear no evil: for thou art with me; thy rod and thy staff
they comfort me.

—Psalm 23:4

When the road into the future looms endlessly dark, remember ancient desert nomads who only traveled in the dark because of the heat during the day. They sewed tiny candleholders on their shoes so they always had enough light for the next step. God is both our light in the darkness and the ingenuity to use it.

August 12

∞

I will greatly rejoice in the Lord, my soul shall be joyful in my
God; for he hath clothed me with the garments of salvation,
he hath covered me with the robe of righteousness, as a
bridegroom decketh himself with ornaments, and as a bride
adorneth herself with her jewels.

—Isaiah 61:10

Sometimes it feel as though our journey is mapped
out. As children we are scheduled, shuttled, and herded.
Adult life falls into a routine we can both rely on and
resent. But every day there is an open road before us,
a path of our choosing marked only by God's love.

August 13

Being confident of this very thing, that he which hath begun a good work in you will perform it until the day of Jesus Christ.

—Philippians 1:6

It's been days since I even considered that I didn't have to be doing all I do alone—pretending to be a superhero. Whew! What a relief to know that God remembered and reminded me. Partnerships are so much better than going it alone.

August 14

*To whom God would make known what is the riches of
the glory of this mystery among the Gentiles;
which is Christ in you, the hope of glory.*

—Colossians 1:27

*B*e enthused, for you hold the key to the life of
your imaginings. That's because God's love for us is not
a mere "consolation prize" we settle for if human love
fails us. (Oh, what a mistaken notion that is!) No, God's
love is the "grand prize." He is the source of all love, and
his love never fails.

August 15

To every thing there is a season, and a time to every purpose under the heaven: A time to be born, and a time to die; a time to plant, and a time to pluck up that which is planted.

—Ecclesiastes 3:1–2

The most simple lesson is the hardest to embody: Our lives are not our own to plan. We live and choose, we love God and family, we work and reify our faith. We fall on hard times and call out to God. We rejoice in our successes and give thanks to God. All things begin and end in God.

August 16

And the life which I now live in the flesh I live by the faith of the Son of God, who loved me, and gave himself for me.
—**Galatians 2:20**

Bless us as we weather this family conflict, Lord. We all have certain needs to be met, certain ways of trying to fulfill our dreams. Yet each of us seeks this one basic thing in the midst of it all: love. Simply love. Remind us that we, too, must sacrifice to move forward in a better life together.

August 17

Lord, thou hast heard the desire of the humble: thou wilt prepare their heart, thou wilt cause thine ear to hear: To judge the fatherless and the oppressed, that the man of the earth may no more oppress.

—Psalm 10:17–18

If we look to service for the earthly benefits it will bring us, we may be disappointed. Yet if we forget about those benefits and gladly serve others, good things happen to us. We are helped in so many ways by those we serve.

August 18

*Then said Jesus to those Jews which believed on him, If ye
continue in my word, then are ye my disciples indeed; And ye
shall know the truth, and the truth shall make you free.*

—**John 8:31–32**

Our joy and sorrow ebb and flow. The scriptures
tell us we cannot even begin to imagine the good
things God has in store for those who love him. Life
the way it was meant to be lived—free from grief and
onus and fear—will overtake us, and we will begin to
truly live at last and forever.

August 19

There is therefore now no condemnation to them which are in Christ Jesus, who walk not after the flesh, but after the Spirit. For the law of the Spirit of life in Christ Jesus hath made me free from the law of sin and death.

—Romans 8:1–2

The promised Messiah—Immanuel, which means "God with us"—was miraculously conceived but born just like any other human baby. It's a great picture of both the glory and humility of God. Even though he could have chosen to continually wow us with his overpowering glory, instead, he gently came alongside us in his humanity, walked in our shoes, carried our sins, and opened the way for us to heaven.

August 20

Rejoicing in hope; patient in tribulation;
continuing instant in prayer.

—Romans 12:12

We see every day the benefits of a "coffee break": at our jobs, from our routines, to catch up with loved ones. But we must also take time to nurture our faith in our daily lives in addition to times of need. To check in with our faith every day, as though it were an old friend, reminds us that God's work is everything.

August 21

And the very God of peace sanctify you wholly; and I pray God your whole spirit and soul and body be preserved blameless unto the coming of our Lord Jesus Christ. Faithful is he that calleth you, who also will do it.

—1 Thessalonians 5:23–24

Perhaps you have a favorite hymn dating from your childhood, or maybe your favorite is one you sing in a church you attend. No matter your acquaintance with that hymn, take a few moments today to look up the lyrics and reflect on them again, allowing your focus on God's faithfulness to lift your heart and mind in gratitude for his unfailing promises and faithful love.

August 22

Jesus Christ the same yesterday, and to day, and for ever.

—Hebrews 13:8

God saw the shepherds kneeling down. God saw the wisest kings bowing with their gifts. God saw the love that night brighter than the brightest star that has ever shone And God saw the baby born that will save the world.

August 23

And the publican, standing afar off, would not lift up so much as his eyes unto heaven, but smote upon his breast, saying, God be merciful to me a sinner.

—Luke 18:13

When we feel the most disappointed in ourselves, it's tempting to question everything. How can anyone love us when we're so disappointing? God loves us despite our sins. For those who love him in return and seek to follow him, his gaze always remains on them, and his heart's intent is to bless and keep them.

August 24

But when the fulness of the time was come, God sent forth his Son, made of a woman, made under the law, To redeem them that were under the law, that we might receive the adoption of sons.

—**Galatians 4:4–5**

The promise to those who believe on Christ is this: You have now passed from a sentence of eternal doom to the certainty of eternal life. Of course, there are conversations that will take place during all our lives around this point, but this is the essence of the gospel. Let's trust God's promise and let the power of the gospel do its work!

August 25

For there is hope of a tree, if it be cut down, that it will sprout again, and that the tender branch thereof will not cease.

—Job 14:7

"Family" means more than just the people who share your bloodline. You need not live in the same house or grow up with the same last name in order to be a family. Our truest loved ones are those with whom we can navigate serious conflicts. Our love may be cut close, but its roots extend deep into our hearts and will survive and grow again.

August 26

For unto us a child is born, unto us a son is given: and the government shall be upon his shoulder: and his name shall be called Wonderful, Counsellor, The mighty God, The everlasting Father, The Prince of Peace.

—Isaiah 9:6

There is a day yet coming when those who belong to God in Christ will be unfettered from the lingering effects of humanity's earthly concerns. Like the promise of Christ himself, this promise survives across the ages and offers hope to us all. We live in God's image in pursuit of this day to come.

August 27

Hope deferred maketh the heart sick: but when the desire cometh, it is a tree of life.

—Proverbs 13:12

Compassion is the ability to walk in another's shoes, even if they are several sizes too small. Compassion is understanding another's challenges, even if they are not our own. Compassion is caring for the welfare of others, even they are different from us. When we share our hearts and minds with those in need, we are greater than the sum of our parts.

August 28

Happy is he that hath the God of Jacob for his help,
whose hope is in the Lord his God.

—Psalm 146:5

$\mathcal{B}$e generous, for you have been given the gift of knowledge by the Lord. You may notice that you and the believers in your life have a spring in their step even on a dull day. Small problems are swept away by the long shadow of the Lord. Large problems are cast in a navigable light.

August 29

But the Lord will be the hope of his people,
and the strength of the children of Israel.

—Joel 3:16

To face our sins and temptations is hard! Many of us don't believe we can commit to a godly life: I could never do that; I can't give this up; I don't want to have to do that. But it is in God that we find the strength to resist temptation. He knows we rely on his example and his holy word.

August 30

For the Lord is good; his mercy is everlasting;
and his truth endureth to all generations.

—Psalm 100:5

Daily life catches up with me, Lord. I worry
about money, my family, and my work. I might have
work responsibilities of my own during the day,
then morph into a "homework helper" and "chief
cook" as soon as I return home from the office. I
wonder what others think of me and question my
choices. But you encourage me to see the biggest
picture of all. Your gifts are the things of heaven,
and thankfully they cannot be touched or taken
away by any earthly concerns.

August 31

*The Lord is good unto them that wait for him, to the soul that
seeketh him. It is good that a man should both hope and
quietly wait for the salvation of the Lord.*

—Lamentations 3:25–26

One of the most trying things our faith can go
through is the trial of waiting for God to intervene for
us in some important way. But waiting patiently for him
to intervene does always not mean the outcome will be
what we'd hoped for. Yes, we must have faith in "things
unseen," but we must also have faith that what we do
see is not the whole story: God's help is bigger than
anything we can comprehend.

September

September 1

∞

Blessed are they that have not seen, and yet have believed.
—John 20:29

When my children were young, they used to wander away sometimes, and I would have trouble finding them for a few moments. As humans we're prone to say "seeing is believing," and I could never rest until I had the little ones in sight again. But this urge is strictly of the earth. Our greatest gift is our ability to think beyond what we see and imagine the possibilities.

September 2

*I thank my God upon every remembrance of you, Always in every
prayer of mine for you all making request with joy.*

—Philippians 1:3–4

After the loss of a loved one we often question God's
motives or even his attention itself. If he were watching,
how could he do this to us? But our beloved friends and
relatives are waiting for us. What we owe to them is what
we owe to God: to live our lives fully and in faith, waiting
for the next step.

September 3

And blessed be his glorious name for ever: and let the whole earth be filled with his glory; Amen, and Amen.

—Psalm 72:19

Be grateful, for through God you have overcome all obstacles. God has given you the life you have and the everlasting life to come; God has given you the strength to do good works, to care for your family, and to foster your faith. He shadows your every action and guides your heart. He listens when you give thanks.

September 4

O give thanks unto the Lord; for he is good.
because his mercy endureth for ever.

—Psalm 118:1

Perhaps God is calling
to you right now to enter
into a conversation with him
about something that has
come between you. He's
open to that meeting and is
merciful and ready to forgive.
He promises to be gracious
to all who come to him with
sincere and humble hearts.

September 5

This also cometh forth from the Lord of hosts, which is wonderful in counsel, and excellent in working.

Isaiah 28:29

Over time we learn that navigating life without God at the helm is an exercise in futility, pain, and trouble. These lessons may come with some pretty hard knocks! But we learn from them that we must turn to God for guidance, and when we do that we learn that he is so good. God is wise and always listening; he is ready to help us choose well for ourselves and those we love.

September 6

Remove far from me vanity and lies: give me neither poverty nor riches.

Proverbs 30:8

There are large ministries now that claim God gives material rewards to the faithful. These assertions are generally materialistic in nature and take scriptures out of context or stretch their meaning beyond recognition. But God's love and salvation have nothing to do with our pride-based image or our earthly status, and our earthly status has nothing to do with our place with God.

September 7

I will praise the name of God with a song,
and will magnify him with thanksgiving.

—Psalm 69:30

For hundreds of years, our greatest artists have devoted themselves to glorifying God. Something about beautiful harmonies or depictions of biblical scenes raises our hearts toward heaven and makes God feel even closer to us. We join forces to express our thanks and love for all to see and hear.

September 8

*Let your conversation be without covetousness;
and be content with such things as ye have: for he hath said,
I will never leave thee, nor forsake thee.*

—Hebrews 13:5

God has given each person a storehouse of wisdom and creativity. But to fully tap into our potential, we have to believe in ourselves—and it helps to know that others believe in us, too. In fact, it can make all the difference. Each person's gifts are different and equally important in God's eyes. We must be our best selves for him.

September 9

And Hannah prayed, and said, My heart rejoiceth in the Lord, mine horn is exalted in the Lord: my mouth is enlarged over mine enemies; because I rejoice in thy salvation.

—1 Samuel 2:1

We can think we're going the right direction, navigating just fine with what we know. But then at some point it dawns on us that we're lost. Stuff doesn't just work out when we're doing our own thing and ignoring God's guidance. But for those of us who are looking to and listening to God, he promises to take our circumstances and use them in our lives for good.

September 10

Happy is the man that findeth wisdom, and the man that getteth understanding. For the merchandise of it is better than the merchandise of silver, and the gain thereof than fine gold.
—**Proverbs 3:13–14**

The greatest lesson my teachers taught me was not on a test sheet or chalkboard, but within my imagination. They made me realize my own potential and opened my eyes to the world of possibilities beyond the classroom walls. Guide me, O God, my lifetime teacher and greatest purveyor of wisdom.

September 11

Although you have not seen [Jesus], you love him; and even though you do not see him now, you believe in him and rejoice with an indescribable and glorious joy.

—1 Peter 1:8 NRSV

The really amazing thing about this promise is that it reveals to us that before we even knew to desire such things in our life with Christ, God knew ahead of time that we would. He already had a plan prepared for us, including all the service we would do in his name, to his honor and glory.

September 12

If any of you lack wisdom, let him ask of God, that giveth to all men liberally, and upbraideth not; and it shall be given him.

—James 1:5

ʟord, hope and optimism are gifts from your hand that can guide me for life. When I struggle to hold hope in my heart, please remind me of it. When I batten down the hatches and prepare for the worst, please let me see that there is a new life around the corner for me. When I can't tap into my own wisdom, please lend me yours. Amen.

September 13

I am the vine, ye are the branches: He that abideth in me,
and I in him, the same bringeth forth much fruit:
for without me ye can do nothing.

—John 15:5

It can seem too good to be true: God has done
all of the work, covered the price of our redemption,
overcoming sin and death for us through Jesus' death
and resurrection. Those who open their hearts to this
gift receive the privilege of being called God's own
children for all eternity. But in turn, we must open
our hearts to him and obey his word.

September 14

But godliness with contentment is great gain. For we brought nothing into this world, and it is certain we can carry nothing out. And having food and raiment let us be therewith content.

– 1 Timothy 6:6–8

Lord, I knew one man who was truly content, a beloved late relative. His life was marked by tragedy and he found comfort and quietude by reflecting on your word. He was the life of every family function, able to enjoy the moment and let go of the past. When he passed, we told countless stories of how he'd graced each of our lives. I think of him every day and strive to find his contentment. Guide me toward peace of mind, Lord. Amen.

September 15

And he shall be like a tree planted by the rivers of water, that bringeth forth his fruit in his season; his leaf also shall not wither; and whatsoever he doeth shall prosper.

—Psalm 1:3

*L*ord, we are the caretakers of our own futures. We must plant and nourish the spiritual seeds that will become tomorrow's garden. Please guide us to pull the weeds of discontent and fertilize with plenty of love so we may grow to be happy and healthy in your word.

September 16

For when God made promise to Abraham, because he could swear
by no greater, he sware by himself, Saying, Surely blessing I will
bless thee, and multiplying I will multiply thee. And so, after
he had patiently endured, he obtained the promise.

—Hebrews 6:13–15

Lord, my kids sometimes do the dumbest things,
skirting disaster. And while it's not possible to put
an old head on young shoulders, O God, I would if I
could. Help me find ways that won't alienate and yet
will protect my impetuous young ones. Help me
remember that they are the greatest blessing.

September 17

For I will not see you now by the way; but I trust to tarry a while with you, if the Lord permit.

—1 Corinthians 16:7

Dear God, today I grew frustrated with my old friend and said some hurtful things. I will pray on it and hope for her forgiveness, and I have faith that you'll help us to mend our friendship. When we find people we love and wish to include in our lives, we must work to hang onto them. Help me to gain compassion and understanding as I resolve the situation.

September 18

How hast thou counselled him that hath no wisdom? and
how hast thou plentifully declared the thing as it is?
—Job 26:3

Finding our way in life is sometimes literal. we're
relying on GPS navigation or directions someone gave us
or maybe even a passenger, and still, we become lost. The
situation can be overwhelming—especially in the dark or
when traffic is zooming in all directions. But God promises
to light our path it we understand where to look, and we
learn lessons from our divergent paths.

September 19

For I will pour water upon him that is thirsty,
and floods upon the dry ground: I will pour my spirit
upon thy seed, and my blessing upon thine offspring.

—Isaiah 44:3–4

I'm always amazed when I see the grown
children I once knew—they are accomplished
adults. But I still see the twinkle in their eyes
of the little ones who created mischief in the
aisles at church or inspired laughter at our
family gatherings. Thank heavens for each
new generation of children, reminding us to
stay young at heart and wonder-filled.

September 20

The Lord hath done great things for us; whereof we are glad.

—Psalm 126:3

God's love is a powerful purveyor of peacefulness.
When we are at peace with God, that feeling radiates like
a ray of sunshine that gives warmth to everything in its
path. Challenges are put in perspective and often more
easily navigated. Obstacles grow smaller or fall away.
Being in harmony with God creates order in our lives.

September 21

∞

So the Lord blessed the latter end of Job more than his beginning.
—Job 42:12

In the midst of a tough time or special trial, we may resent the emotional and mental space these efforts take up. But they are spiritual blessings that show themselves in our growing character, in our relationship with God, in the fruit of our service to him. By turning to him in our neediest moments, we grow closer to him and more spiritually whole.

September 22

For the Lord thy God bringeth thee into a good land, a land of brooks of water, of fountains and depths that spring out of valleys and hills; A land of wheat, and barley, and vines, and fig trees, and pomegranates; a land of oil olive, and honey; A land wherein thou shalt eat bread without scarceness, thou shalt not lack any thing in it.

—Deuteronomy 8:7–9

While God is not a "name it and claim it" God, he is a God of his word, and as we walk closely with him, we will know how to pray with confidence. He promises to provide a bounty for us if we commit to a godly life. In exchange for giving up the illusion of control over our lives on earth, we receive spiritual abundance.

September 23

And I will make them and the places round about my hill a blessing; and I will cause the shower to come down in his season; there shall be showers of blessing.

—Ezekiel 34:26

Every now and then, think like a grandparent instead of a parent. Let your kids have ice cream for breakfast. Go ahead and buy that little toy they want in the supermarket. Have a good, long cuddle like you don't see them everyday. We are blessed with love and may freely express it.

September 24

Come, and let us return unto the Lord: for he hath torn, and he will heal us; he hath smitten, and he will bind us up.

—Hosea 6:1

God's promises in this passage point to a divine heart that longs to be kind and merciful. God still calls us into relationship with himself today—into dialogue that will heal our perspective and reconcile us fully to him. We may bring our feelings of hurt or confusion to him and discuss them openly in order to patch our relationship and move forward.

September 25

In your book were written all the days that were formed for me, when none of them as yet existed.

—Psalm 139:16 NRSV

When I think about scraped knees and bruised hearts I think about you, Lord, for soothing my earliest hurts. You have helped me all the days of my life through adolescence, adulthood, and having a family of my own. I feel comforted that you have a plan for me, and that knowledge frees me to live my life with vibrancy and love. Thank you for the gift of this life I live.

September 26

∞

For he clave to the Lord, and departed not from following him, but kept his commandments, which the Lord commanded Moses. And the Lord was with him; and he prospered whithersoever he went forth.

—2 Kings 18:6–7

Recovering from a professional setback is hard work. It's costly not only in financial terms but more significantly in terms of the toll it takes on one's hopes and desires and longings. But God promises us spiritual prosperity in his word.

September 27

Now therefore, our God, we thank thee,
and praise thy glorious name.

—1 Chronicles 29:13

Like piecing together a quilt of leftovers, rescuing birds, or forging truces, mothers tend to preserve and create rather than throw away or fight. I learned this mindset from my own mother but it represents important biblical truths to me. When we create and preserve, we honor God's creation with our works. When we strike an accord, we love and forgive.

September 28

Now unto him that is able to keep you from falling,
and to present you faultless before the presence of his
glory with exceeding joy.

—Jude 1:24–25

This passage is a benediction, a blessing that Jude, the brother of Jesus, wrote to those who would read his brief letter. Perhaps Jude is harkening back to the Psalms when he writes this blessing. There we find assurances that even though a person pursuing God's ways may trip along the path, they will not fall headlong—God's own hand upholds those who trust in him. What a comforting word!

September 29

I am the door: by me if any man enter in, he shall be saved,
and shall go in and out, and find pasture.

—John 10:9

Sunday school children used to sing a song with these lyrics: "One door and only one, and yet its sides are two / Inside and outside, on which side are you?" It's a reference to this passage where Jesus tells his listeners in metaphor that he is the way by which we can be reconciled to the Father. He is the door to restored relationship with God. There is no other means.

September 30

I will praise thee; for I am fearfully and wonderfully made: marvellous are thy works; and that my soul knoweth right well.

—Psalm 139:14

Lord, thank you for this body I live in. Each feature has a story of service to my health and well being; each scar a lesson learned or even a now-fond memory. As I bend to pick up a child, whisk a meringue by hand, or reach for the high shelf, I marvel at how functional this creation is.

October

October 1

∞

But ask now the beasts, and they shall teach thee; and the fowls of the air, and they shall tell thee.

—Job 12:7

Dear Lord, the miracles of creation astonish me. Nature's abundance is a marvel every day: the cycle of seasons, the way the trees go dormant and reemerge each year. My yard is filled with beautiful living things. They have a place all their own in my treasure chest of memories.

October 2

I therefore, the prisoner of the Lord, beseech you that ye walk worthy of the vocation wherewith ye are called, With all lowliness and meekness, with longsuffering, forbearing one another in love; Endeavouring to keep the unity of the Spirit in the bond of peace.

—Ephesians 4:1–3

God does not challenge us beyond our means to cope. He knows that heart disease and cancer aren't what stand in the way of our most serious need—we must overcome our doubts in him. Once we walk in faith, we can approach our obstacles with the same humility with which we approach our relationship with God.

October 3

And this commandment have we from him,
That he who loveth God love his brother also.

—1 John 4:21

here is some part of us that still wants the little fix of fleeting pleasure or relief or escape that sin provides. One of the most tempting is to hold grudges or rise in angry response, though we know so clearly that God tells us to love one another unconditionally. But the same as we don't sustain anger at God over something we can't understand, we must let go of anger at our brothers.

October 4

And be not drunk with wine, wherein is excess; but be filled with the Spirit; Speaking to yourselves in psalms and hymns and spiritual songs, singing and making melody in your heart to the Lord; Giving thanks always for all things unto God and the Father in the name of our Lord Jesus Christ.

—Ephesians 5:18–20

God's advice to us is plain and clear. It's not that we're automatons and God has a program we'd be plugged into to serve him—he wants us to understand what's expected of us and see clearly the path to salvation.

October 5

But with me it is a very small thing that I should be judged of you, or of man's judgment: yea, I judge not mine own self.

—1 Corinthians 4:3

Dear Lord, I've always struggled to see my younger sibling as an independent adult. Whenever I crave ice cream sundaes and cotton candy, I remember the times we shared and am transported back to childhood. But we're all adults now and the family home is long behind us as we make families of our own. Help me to see my sibling as a peer and an equal, deserving of my respect as much as of my love.

October 6

Let him know, that he which converteth the sinner from the error of his way shall save a soul from death, and shall hide a multitude of sins.

—James 5:20

Our influence on others matters, especially when it's spiritual. The scriptures reveal to us that God has placed eternity in the hearts of humanity—both eternal life and the awareness of it. After all, why do people strive to please and appease various gods? What is this thing in us that knows right from wrong? These are not survival-of-the-fittest instincts. God has, indeed, built eternity into our being.

October 7

According as his divine power hath given unto us all things that pertain unto life and godliness, through the knowledge of him that hath called us to glory and virtue.

—2 Peter 1:3

When we think of things like glory and virtue, they can seem like a style of clothes we admire but think we can't wear because they "just aren't us." Glory and virtue, the things we attribute to Christ! But we need to understand that Jesus wants to share all that is his with us. He wants us to rule and reign in heaven with him for eternity. And as we grow in him here and now, he has provided everything we need for life and godliness.

October 8

Whereby are given unto us exceeding great and precious promises: that by these ye might be partakers of the divine nature, having escaped the corruption that is in the world through lust.

—2 Peter 1:4

Exceeding, great, precious. These words speak of overwhelming abundance, of profound importance, of something held dear. These are the words the apostle Peter used to describe God's promises to us. And yet, do we take time to reflect upon and realize the treasures that they are? These promises! May we perceive their worth, and give God due thanks and praise for his goodness toward us.

October 9

The Lord is not slack concerning his promise, as some men
count slackness; but is longsuffering to us-ward, not willing
that any should perish, but that all should come to repentance.

—2 Peter 3:9

"Why doesn't God just set the world straight?!"
Sometimes when we see evil and injustice, that's how
we feel. God reminds us here that there will come a day
when he does just that—but that day will also be the
end of opportunities to turn to him. It will be the end
of time and the beginning of eternity; a time of giving
account to him; a joyous time for all who belong to him;
and a dreadful time for all who have rejected him.

October 10

Nevertheless we, according to his promise, look for new heavens and a new earth, wherein dwelleth righteousness.

—2 Peter 3:13

What will it be like—the new heavens and new earth? We have some descriptions in God's word, but they are metaphors. The realities will be the unveiling of a prototype never even remotely imagined. But what will be even more remarkable is the absence of unrighteousness—the reality of living where there is only what is right and true and good. We will never have to be guarded, to be skeptical, to watch our back, or to wait for even the first shoe to drop.

October 11

He that abideth in the doctrine of Christ,
he hath both the Father and the Son.

—2 John 1:9

In Jeremiah 31, God told his people that one day he would establish a new covenant with them. It's the only place the words "new covenant" appear in the Old Testament. Now, fast forward. As Jesus held up one of the Passover cups at the Last Supper, he said, "This is the new covenant in my blood." He was telling them that he embodied the promise made by the God in Jeremiah.

October 12

Are not five sparrows sold for two farthings, and not one of them is forgotten before God? But even the very hairs of your head are all numbered. Fear not therefore: ye are of more value than many sparrows.

—Luke 12:6–7

We are precious in God's eyes, as is the tiniest part of his creation. Does that mean everything's going to go our way? Not at all. But it does mean that we can feel reassured that someone is watching us, someone cares what happens to us, and someone wants to light our way.

October 13

Most men will proclaim every one his own goodness:
but a faithful man who can find?

—Proverbs 20:6

It's just plain hard to watch law-flouters sitting fat and happy in all the bounty their crimes have garnered them. But even as the laments hang in the air, you can almost hear the divine "Wait for it . . . " Sometimes it's hard to wait, but it helps to remember that no one who refuses to repent from their evil is getting away with anything.

October 14

For we know that if our earthly house of this tabernacle were dissolved, we have a building of God, an house not made with hands, eternal in the heavens.

—2 Corinthians 5:1

Because of what Jesus did on the cross to reconcile us to the Father, we can pray, "Our Father, who art in heaven . . ." Jesus said in John 10:30, "I and my Father are one." That is why to embrace Christ is to know both him and the Father. Through Christ we know eternal life in the kingdom of God.

October 15

I say unto you, Love your enemies, bless them that curse you, do good to them that hate you, and pray for them which despitefully use you, and persecute you; That ye may be the children of your Father which is in heaven: for he maketh his sun to rise on the evil and on the good, and sendeth rain on the just and on the unjust.

—Matthew 5:43–45

This is the tallest order in God's word: to love our enemies. But as we live in ways that reveal our trust in God's saving grace and that demonstrate genuine love to others, God promises that his Spirit will work through us to point people to Christ—to his grace that will save them, too, from the dark powers of sin and death, if they are willing to receive it from him.

October 16

Blessed are the merciful: for they shall obtain mercy.

—Matthew 5:7

This blessing holds implicit promises that can give us much-needed assurances as we make our way along life's path. We all make mistakes, and we are all on the receiving end of the mistakes of others. God urges us to be merciful that we all may benefit from that mercy both as giver and recipient. Through this reciprocation we feel compassion for one another.

October 17

Just as water reflects the face,
so one human heart reflects another.
—Proverbs 27:19 NRSV

*L*ord, I have found my soulmate. Thank you for helping me do that, and thank you for bringing me a person whose values and spirit and mind reflect my own. As we walk forward into a life together, I know I learn new things every day because of this love. Having someone who feels like home to me protects me as I venture out into the world with an open heart.

October 18

He that despiseth his neighbour sinneth:
but he that hath mercy on the poor, happy is he.

—Proverbs 14:21

Not everyone seems worthy of our love. Some sin against each other without a second thought. They are not looking out for our well being. They are not going to be willing to put our interests above their own if they feel cornered or trapped in their wrongdoing. But to hate is a sin, pure and simple, and those we are tempted to hate are often simply poor in spirit. The only way to bring them to God is to love them first and foremost.

October 19

Now unto the King eternal, immortal, invisible, the only wise God, be honour and glory for ever and ever. Amen.

—1 Timothy 1:17

Some may balk at Jesus Christ's claim as the only God, King of Kings. He backed it up with the sacrifice of his own life and the payment of our sin debt, and he rose from the dead just as he said he would. That is why we can trust that he truly is the door through which we can enter the promise of eternal life. There is no other.

October 20

For in thee, O Lord, do I hope: thou wilt hear, O Lord my God.
—Psalm 38:15

When we feel weighed down by earthly troubles, we should look to the heavens. We won't wake up to a list of undone things that weigh on us. There will not be a dreaded dentist appointment or cancer diagnosis. All that will be past. Our new home, where only righteousness dwells, is God's promise to all who love him and await his coming.

October 21

I delight to do thy will, O my God:
yea, thy law is within my heart.

—Psalm 40:8

While we don't understand all the ins and outs of how God will deal with all of the reckoning that must take place, we know he will do so with perfect righteousness and justice and with finality. God sees that day and all that it will entail, and in his mercy, he holds back his promise of final judgment, desiring that people escape and be saved.

October 22

But God, who is rich in mercy, for his great love wherewith he loved us, Even when we were dead in sins, hath quickened us together with Christ, by grace ye are saved.

—**Ephesians 2:4–5**

On the day of judgment, the Lord is able to present us faultless before his throne in glory. How can that be? We're full of imperfections! It's only because on that day, Christ will credit his own righteous life as a gift to those who have entrusted themselves to him. He wants to provide the very best that can be given—not just life, but abundant life.

October 23

But ye, beloved, building up yourselves on your most holy faith,
praying in the Holy Ghost, Keep yourselves in the love of God,
looking for the mercy of our Lord Jesus Christ unto eternal life.
—Jude 1:20–21

Why am I so contrary? I wonder and worry. Perhaps it is tiredness or frustration but too often I lose my cool and then the children do likewise until we have a mess and muddle. A meeting ran late; I was late picking up my son at basketball practice and felt guilty and anxious. I snapped at him; I snapped at my husband. I'm so grateful that God can help repair it.

October 24

And of some have compassion, making a difference:
And others save with fear, pulling them out of the fire;
hating even the garment spotted by the flesh.
—Jude 1:22–23

Time-outs are equally good for cranky adults as for disobedient children, sending us to a quiet place to think about our actions, attitudes, and moods. And in that quiet moment, an intervening God comes to hold and inspire us to better days ahead.

October 25

For ye are all the children of God by faith in Christ Jesus. For as many of you as have been baptized into Christ have put on Christ.

—Galatians 3:26–27

$\mathscr{E}$ven in the face of struggles and difficulties, there is a higher order of goodness at work in our lives. We may not be able to physically detect it at all times, but our faith knows the truth, and the truth sets us free.

October 26

There is neither Jew nor Greek, there is neither bond nor free, there is neither male nor female: for ye are all one in Christ Jesus. And if ye be Christ's, then are ye Abraham's seed, and heirs according to the promise.
—Galatians 3:28–29

We have his Word, the Bible; we have his indwelling presence, his Spirit; we have our fellow believers, his body, the church; we have been equipped to serve him, his spiritual gifts. All of these things are promised to us that we might "grow into" and one day realize his eternal call to glory and virtue in and through Christ Jesus.

October 27

When they shall go, I will spread my net upon them; I will bring them down as the fowls of the heaven; I will chastise them, as their congregation hath heard.

--Hosea 7:12

God may throw us a few curves in life—we may feel hassled, troubled, anxious, or uncomfortable, and not understand why our circumstances don't fit our desires. But if we trust in the wisdom of his plan, God will provide for all our needs.

October 28

Woe unto them! for they have fled from me: destruction unto them! because they have transgressed against me: though I have redeemed them, yet they have spoken lies against me.

—Hosea 7:13

No one knows the mind of God, nor why he chooses to work the way he does. But in our most difficult circumstances, we will miss the peace of his presence unless we persevere in trusting that he is always faithful and always good. His word is clear, we must only embrace it.

October 29

For a bishop must be blameless, as the steward of God; not
selfwilled, not soon angry, not given to wine, no striker,
not given to filthy lucre; But a lover of hospitality,
a lover of good men, sober, just, holy, temperate.

—Titus 1:7–8

God, I confess I struggle to be the person you know
I can be. While it's easy not to strike another in anger,
it's much harder to rewire my temper in the first
place. But I do my best to be generous to others and
set a good example, and I know you'll be on my side
as I work over a lifetime to become a better me.

October 30

*They profess that they know God; but in works
they deny him, being abominable, and disobedient,
and unto every good work reprobate.*

—Titus 1:16

Dear Lord, help me turn away from insidious false prophets. It seems like every day brings a new story of one of your servants committing a terrible crime, using your good word or authority to take advantage. I know I have a good head on my shoulders and hope I can sniff out these impostors to your word.

October 31

For even when we were with you, this we commanded you,
that if any would not work, neither should he eat. For we hear
that there are some which walk among you disorderly,
working not at all, but are busybodies.

—2 Thessalonians 3:10–11

Lord, I want to leave the fighting behind us and
get back to the business of life. It's time to begin the
healing process and stop the pettiness and gossiping.
Show me how to reconcile and how to be humble
without being a doormat—I want the respect we
have had for one another to remain intact. Amen.

November

November 1

Yet count him not as an enemy, but admonish him as a brother.

—2 Thessalonians 3:15

Thank you, my friend, for the love you never fail to offer, the help you never fail to give, and the compassion you offer with your guidance. Without you, my life would be half empty. With you, I feel happy, whole, and complete. I know you'll support me no matter what.

November 2

Remembering without ceasing your work of faith, and labour
of love, and patience of hope in our Lord Jesus Christ,
in the sight of God and our Father.

—1 Thessalonians 1:3

As children, we often get
annoyed by our mother's
constant attention and doting.
But once we become adults
with children of our own, we
realize we had been blessed
with the greatest gift of all—
the unconditional love only
a mother can give.

November 3

And they sang together by course in praising and giving thanks unto the Lord; because he is good, for his mercy endureth for ever toward Israel. And all the people shouted with a great shout, when they praised the Lord, because the foundation of the house of the Lord was laid.

—Ezra 3:11

Coming together in worship with prayer, song, and psalm makes us expectant people. Here we find what we came seeking: your abiding, ever-present daily love. We leave, blessed with the truth that it goes with us into the rest of our lives.

November 4

If there come any unto you, and bring not this doctrine, receive him not into your house, neither bid him God speed: For he that biddeth him God speed is partaker of his evil deeds.

—2 John 1:10–11

Good friends keep us accountable to what is right and good. If we're willing to reciprocate—at the risk of hurting our friend—then we are a good friend in return. As God tells us here, to let an ill deed go unchecked is to become a participant.

November 5

Beloved, thou doest faithfully whatsoever thou doest to the brethren, and to strangers; We therefore ought to receive such, that we might be fellowhelpers to the truth.

—3 John 1:5, 8

Galvanize me into prevention, intervention, and rebuilding your world, creator God. Kids need fixers, not just worriers and those prone to panic. They need to hear plans, not just alarms. Let hope, not fear, be the last word in the bedtime stories I tell.

November 6

For we have not followed cunningly devised fables, when we made known unto you the power and coming of our Lord Jesus Christ, but were eyewitnesses of his majesty.

—2 Peter 1:16

All the world moves to a rhythm so large that our small perspective can barely take it in. Occasionally when we run into a moment of clarity, seeing beyond and above ourselves, we catch the beat and hear clearly the word of God. The enormity of his word overwhelms us and fills us with the holy spirit.

November 7

Therefore if any man be in Christ, he is a new creature: old things are passed away; behold, all things are become new

—Isaiah 1:17

God sent his son as a sacrifice and as a pattern for his followers. As you look at your own life, how might you strive to be more Christlike? How might you inspire others to greater heights in their own loving, advocacy, and forgiveness?

November 8

Therefore thou art inexcusable, O man, whosoever thou art that judgest: for wherein thou judgest another, thou condemnest thyself; for thou that judgest doest the same things.

—Psalm 9:1

*L*ord, the way I respond to things in my life is so important. Loved ones who make mistakes need comfort first of all, not judgment, and it's tempting to try to sneak both into that first conversation. Everyone makes mistakes; tomorrow may be my time to do so. Help me tap into my compassion first and foremost.

November 9

Then Peter said unto them, Repent, and be baptized every one of you in the name of Jesus Christ for the remission of sins, and ye shall receive the gift of the Holy Ghost.

--Acts 2.38

Parents have the opportunity be the guiding light for their children. We can talk about all of the assurances--both for the present time and for eternity--that God has given to us. Just the promise of eternal life, even without all the other kind and tender mercies God pledges to provide to those who love and trust him, is beyond what we could have hoped.

November 10

For the promise is unto you, and to your children, and to all that are afar off, even as many as the Lord our God shall call.

—Acts 2:39

There is no ocean so wide that someone can't sail it. There is no mountain so tall that someone can't scale it. There is no task so arduous that someone can't teach it. There is no dream so impossible that someone can't reach it.

November 11

Then Peter said, Silver and gold have I none; but such as I have give I thee: In the name of Jesus Christ of Nazareth rise up and walk. And he leaping up stood, and walked, and entered with them into the temple, walking, and leaping, and praising God.

—Acts 3:6; 8

Lord, I've caught glimpses of your glory and I know the depth of your righteousness, but today I feel sad and doubtful. I turned to the story of the man made to walk again by the hand of Jesus Christ and felt your love and power well up within me. Thank you for your miracles and for guiding me to them as I face my own challenges.

November 12

If we live in the Spirit, let us also walk in the Spirit.
Let us not be desirous of vain glory,
provoking one another, envying one another.
—Galatians 5:25–26

Progress in the folds of a family, O God, is not a straight, flat line but rather ups and downs. From day to day, our attitudes shift and change, we act badly toward one another and then forgive. Our rhythms overlap and move apart but we must all take the long view of our great growth and love. Give me energy and patience to go with the flow.

November 13

Bear ye one another's burdens, and so fulfil the law of Christ.
For if a man think himself to be something, when he is
nothing, he deceiveth himself.

—Galatians 6:2–3

Sometimes we put up a false front, even with our closest friends and loved ones. We think, "What would happen if they knew what's really going on with me?" But our families want to help us shoulder our heaviest weights! When we stop hiding behind a "happy face," we open the door to true intimacy.

November 14

Do all things without murmurings and disputings: That ye may be blameless and harmless, the sons of God, without rebuke, in the midst of a crooked and perverse nation, among whom ye shine as lights in the world.

—Philippians 2:14–15

Dear God, I love to feed my friends. The fare doesn't have to be gourmet to bring joy into the hearts about our tables. Rather, generous portions of laughter and fellowship nourish our table guests by exposing them to love and assuring them of their special places in our lives.

November 15

Brethren, I count not myself to have apprehended: but this one thing I do, forgetting those things which are behind, and reaching forth unto those things which are before, I press toward the mark for the prize of the high calling of God in Christ Jesus.

—Philippians 3:13–14

How is it that the lonesome echo of a loon across a deep, blue lake at dusk restores such a sense of inner calmness to my spirit? Maybe it's because I slow down long enough to see my reflection and remember who created me.

November 16

That their hearts might be comforted, being knit together in love, and unto all riches of the full assurance of understanding, to the acknowledgement of the mystery of God, and of the Father, and of Christ; In whom are hid all the treasures of wisdom and knowledge.

—Colossians 2:2–3

What a wonderful day! And now, God of rest and peace, the children are sleeping, replete with the joys of our autumn discoveries that they are savoring to the last drop. We celebrate the joy of ordinary days and rest in your care.

November 17

Set your affection on things above, not on things on the
earth. For ye are dead, and your life is hid with Christ
in God. When Christ, who is our life, shall appear,
then shall ye also appear with him in glory.

—Colossians 3:2–4

Nothing, not even death, was beyond Jesus Christ's
power to overcome in life. And not long after, Jesus
himself would ultimately conquer our great foe, death,
by rising from the grave, providing the promise of
resurrection for all who trust in him.

November 18

For the law having a shadow of good things to come, and not the very image of the things, can never with those sacrifices which they offered year by year continually make the comers thereunto perfect. For then would they not have ceased to be offered?

—Hebrews 10:1–2

Thank you, Lord of patience, for every day's new chance to take a step forward. If we were perfect, we would not need your redemption. I see the shadow of good things to come.

November 19

For if we sin wilfully after that we have received the knowledge of the truth, there remaineth no more sacrifice for sins, But a certain fearful looking for of judgment and fiery indignation, which shall devour the adversaries.

—Hebrews 10:26–27

In a pinch, we hope to choose righteously. It's the wisdom of self preservation that guides such decisions. And it's that same kind of wisdom that kicks in for us once we've had some education in the school of hard knocks. God is there to support us every day, the same way that he sees every indiscretion. We can only try to balance the ledger!

November 20

But we are not of them who draw back unto perdition;
but of them that believe to the saving of the soul.

—Hebrews 10:39

We all know a "shrinking violet," someone who shies away from attention. But being a Christian means doing the opposite. Who made a bigger splash in history than Jesus Christ? It's important to stand confidently in your faith and embrace it with your whole heart. To shy away from the message or what it means in your life is to shirk God's teachings.

November 21

We have dealt very corruptly against thee, and have not kept the commandments, nor the statutes, nor the judgments, which thou commandedst thy servant Moses.

Nehemiah 1:7

Nehemiah observed the sins of his people and went to great lengths to right those sins and honor God. We can all benefit from this example: No situation is ever so bad that we can't reach out to God for help and guidance. We even have his written instructions on how best to live our lives, love one another, and honor him. It's time to fess up and confront whatever is on your mind in order to move on with God's help.

November 22

Remember me, O my God, for good.
—**Nehemiah 13:31**

Our relationship with God is both infinite and extremely personal. We revere him with our words and actions and faith and he in turn effects change in our lives and those of our loved ones. There is never a time when God isn't listening, never a time when our commitment to him is lost in the shuffle. We can count on him to remember our names and recognize our hearts.

November 23

Let us search and try our ways, and turn again to the Lord.
Let us lift up our heart with our hands unto God in the heavens.

—Lamentations 3:40

It's a common problem that we ask God for help when we're in trouble but can sometimes pass him by when we're doing well. But it's always the right time to ask yourself how you feel about your relationship with God. Lamentations pictures a worst-case scenario of desolation and despair, but even so, it ends with a faithful, open-hearted appeal to God for help.

November 24

Ye shall not respect persons in judgment; but ye shall hear the small as well as the great; ye shall not be afraid of the face of man; for the judgment is God's.

—Deuteronomy 1:17

Lord, today I slighted one of my children without meaning to. I didn't listen when she offered her opinion, and she wondered if I dismissed her as being "just a kid." Everyone is special and everyone has valid input to offer. It's my responsibility to raise my children to be confident, thoughtful people! My daughter forgave me with great poise—I am as proud of her as I am embarrassed for myself. Thank you, God, for the blessing of her sweet personality and growing presence of mind.

November 25

Seek ye the Lord, all ye meek of the earth, which have wrought his judgment; seek righteousness, seek meekness: it may be ye shall be hid in the day of the Lord's anger.

—Zephaniah 2:3

God is great and God is good, but we must all still pay great heed to the coming day of judgment. It's impossible to fly under God's radar, so to be "hidden" here implies obedience and a willingness to yield to God's word. Even those who sinned against Israel in the Old Testament are offered a glimmer of hope by Zephaniah: a possible chance to stand placidly among the righteous on Judgment Day.

November 26

*The Lord thy God in the midst of thee is mighty; he will save,
he will rejoice over thee with joy; he will rest in his love,
he will joy over thee with singing.*

—Zephaniah 3:17

Dear Lord, thank you for this fine day. My family was at their cooperative, loving best; my coworkers worked together on a project we can all be proud of. I owe you everything I have but find that I don't say it often enough. These beautiful days of consequence are the light of my life and I am so grateful. I've lived to see your sovereignty. You've taught my knees to bow.

November 27

Thus saith the Lord of hosts; Consider your ways.

—Haggai 1:7

Gently, Lord, love me gently on this tough day. I'm hurting now because of my own mistake. It's nothing serious, but it especially hurts to know I brought the pain upon myself and disappointed you. The silver lining is that I know how to resolve the situation. Lord, I love that your word and my own feelings coincide when it comes to knowing right from wrong, even if I sometimes ignore my better judgment. Thank you for welcoming me back into the fold every time without fail.

November 28

And I will shake all nations, and the desire of all nations shall come: and I will fill this house with glory, saith the Lord of hosts.

—Haggai 2:7

The love of God has made me strong, true, and kind. I am confident in all I do because of the Lord. His word has made me free and joyful. I believe in myself as his servant, and I may act boldly to preserve and uphold his message of love and goodwill. We call it "self esteem," but I know what I have is esteem for myself as part of God's creation. May I act accordingly every day of my life.

November 29

Having confidence in thy obedience I wrote unto thee,
knowing that thou wilt also do more than I say.

—Philemon 1:21

The apostle Paul faced many hardships in his missionary journeys. He was beaten, shipwrecked, and left for dead. Finally he was imprisoned in Rome to await trial, and it is believed he was executed under Emperor Nero's rule. During this imprisonment, Paul wrote heartfelt entreaties using the message of Jesus Christ. He never rested from his life's work of teaching and advocating God's word, even when he faced the greatest possible obstacles and pain.

November 30

I thank my God, making mention of thee always in my prayers, Hearing of thy love and faith, which thou hast toward the Lord Jesus, and toward all saints; That the communication of thy faith may become effectual by the acknowledging of every good thing which is in you in Christ Jesus.

—Philemon 1:4–6

In the self-help age, we're exposed to many messages about habits: how to make them, how to break them, what's too much, what's too little? The way to build a relationship with God is simple: Believe wholeheartedly in the power and glory of Jesus Christ. By professing this belief and sitting with it every day, our relationship with God will grow richer, deeper, and more meaningful. Paul thanks God for Philemon's loving commitment to God's word and for Philemon's sincere efforts to live in God's goodwill.

December

December 1

For every house is builded by some man;
but he that built all things is God.

—Hebrews 3:4

The Bible is itself a miracle. It's a volume of 66 books with more than 40 authors written over a span of about 1,500 years. And miraculously it all hangs together—the first testament pointing to the coming of Christ, and the second testament revealing Christ, his atonement, the start of his church, and the revelation of what will happen at the end of the age. Within this framework, the Bible is full of God's wisdom and instruction, providing his promised guidance and encouragement for life.

December 2

Take heed, brethren, lest there be in any of you an evil heart of unbelief, in departing from the living God. But exhort one another daily, while it is called To day; lest any of you be hardened through the deceitfulness of sin.

—Hebrews 3:12–13

The cornerstone of the twelve-step recovery model is to admit that we can't control our worst impulses and must entrust our care to a higher power. To be accountable, we first need to find someone to be accountable to! Faith is the same for those who aren't in crisis: profess and nurture our faith daily; don't let our doubts or fears fester; and trust wholly in God.

December 3

Seeing then that we have a great high priest, that is passed into the heavens, Jesus the Son of God, let us hold fast our profession.

—Hebrews 4:14

The first generations of Christians had the crucifixion and resurrection of Jesus Christ on their minds as recent history. They still lived in the same environment where it happened, and it didn't take long for serious persecution of Christians to spread widely. But then, as now, believers knew they had the savior on their side. Belief promised an earthly life of fellowship and enrichment, despite the troubles, and an eternal life beyond imagination.

December 4

For we have not an high priest which cannot be touched with the feeling of our infirmities; but was in all points tempted like as we are, yet without sin.

—Hebrews 4:15

Yes, to live a godly life can be intimidating. In tired times, we frame it to ourselves as a life of difficult purity and self-denial. But we have a great role model in Jesus Christ, whose time on earth was spent with a diverse and challenging population in many different places. He walked among us and understood the temptations all around but was able to persevere! Every day is a new chance to strive to be Christlike in our thoughts and actions.

December 5

Let us therefore come boldly unto the throne of grace, that we may obtain mercy, and find grace to help in time of need.

—Hebrews 4:16

One of the greatest comforts of God's family is the knowledge that God has a plan. We can resist and twist in the wind but ultimately will find our way back into his arms, and he will welcome us with love and forgiveness. Life sometimes treats us kindly and sometimes harshly, but God loves and watches out for us forever.

December 6

For unto us was the gospel preached, as well as unto them: but the word preached did not profit them, not being mixed with faith in them that heard it.

—Hebrews 4:2

Dear God, I'm frustrated with my teenager, who told me that he won't be coming to church with me anymore because he's not sure he believes in you. I know his feelings will ebb and flow as he grows into an adult and I know I will persevere in my faith no matter what, but how could this happen? Help me to see that this setback is probably temporary. Challenges to faith can only make that faith stronger in the end. Critical thinking is not an obstacle. Thank you, God.

December 7

Blessed is the man that endureth temptation: for when he is tried, he shall receive the crown of life, which the Lord hath promised to them that love him.

—James 1:12

To spend my life with God is a choice I freely make. To love God and let God love me is the light of my life— what enables me to choose wisely and be thoughtful to those around me. God empowers me to resist temptation in the same breath that he compels me to give generously of myself and my resources. The blessing that James promises feels to me like God's love: it shines on me every day, lights the darkness, and illuminates my path.

December 8

Wherefore, my beloved brethren, let every man be swift to hear, slow to speak, slow to wrath: For the wrath of man worketh not the righteousness of God.

—James 1:19–20

One of the toughest things I taught my children was to listen and hear. Many of us do so by putting our feet in our mouths once we've hurt a friend's feelings or wounded with our words. At those times it's critical to open my heart and hear what is on my friend's mind, so I can resolve the issue and remind my friend how much I care. Anger won't solve any problem, and anger will never impress God.

December 9

If any man among you seem to be religious, and bridleth not his tongue, but deceiveth his own heart, this man's religion is vain.

—James 1:26

$\mathcal{L}$ord, the other day in traffic someone cut me off— the license plate read "BLESSED." I apologize to you for my initial vocal reaction, but it gave me a great idea. What if we all acted as though we wore our status as Christians on our sleeves for all to see? Not only would we be accountable to you, but we'd be accountable to the reputation of good Christians everywhere. We are blessed and should spread that blessing in the world. God, help me to choose the high road. Amen.

December 10

For whosoever shall keep the whole law,
and yet offend in one point, he is guilty of all.

—James 2:10

Following God is not a fad diet; there are no "cheat days." In fact, on those days when it's most challenging to live a just and godly life, we must dig even deeper to stay true to ourselves and to God. To be good when there are no obstacles means little compared to how we act under duress.

December 11

For as the body without the spirit is dead,
so faith without works is dead also.

—James 2:26

Dear God, help me never to be a "Sunday Christian." It's easy to think our busy lives excuse us from some obligations. After all, aren't going to work and raising families worthy pursuits in God's eyes? But every day there are opportunities to speak to God with my actions and I need to make the most of those moments.

December 12

But the wisdom that is from above is first pure, then peaceable, gentle, and easy to be intreated, full of mercy and good fruits, without partiality, and without hypocrisy.

—James 3:17

This simple verse explains many things about God's love. It soothes our souls and frees us to do our best work. It guides us to righteousness and rewards us for complying. It is a complete behavioral and moral code from which we may all benefit.

December 13

And the Lord said, I have pardoned according to thy word:
But as truly as I live, all the earth shall be filled
with the glory of the Lord.

—Numbers 14:20–21

Lord, the best way I know to say thank you for your wonderful guidance is to try to be the kind of person you have taught me to be. Please continue to lift me up every day as I strive to be my best self.

December 14

And now, behold, we are in thine hand: as it seemeth good and right unto thee to do unto us, do.
—Joshua 9:25

Each of us has our own angels to guide and direct us: A beloved friend, a trusted mentor, or a family member we can always depend on. Angels are everywhere. Joshua is a trusted hand of God through his works and he serves as one of these angels to those who follow him. They trust him to relay the word of God and guide them righteously.

December 15

And they told him, and said, We came unto the land whither thou sentest us, and surely it floweth with milk and honey; and this is the fruit of it.

—**Numbers 13:27**

My prized possession in all the world is nothing that can be held or shown—it is the faith that I have nurtured and tended during my life, my personal land of milk and honey. Thank you, God, for the soil, the water, and the sunlight that have helped me to grow.

December 16

Talk no more so exceeding proudly; let not arrogancy come out of your mouth: for the Lord is a God of knowledge, and by him actions are weighed.

—1 Samuel 2:3

*L*ord, nothing is more humbling than the loved ones who've known me for my whole life. When I catch up with my siblings and cousins, we are anchored by memories of silly childhood choices and even serious adult mistakes. What a blessing it is to have people in my life with whom I share so much history and so many special memories; who forgive me and sees the whole person I am.

December 17

And Gideon said unto them, I will not rule over you, neither shall my son rule over you: the Lord shall rule over you.

—Judges 8:23

The people defer to powerful Gideon and offer to follow his word, but he knows that God is the true leader. Let us never forget during our successes that they are never ours alone. Not only are we supported and aided by our friends, colleagues, or loved ones—we are all the children of God and subject to his will. Nothing happens without his blessing.

December 18

*And Moses cried unto the Lord, saying, Heal her now,
O God, I beseech thee.*

—Numbers 12:13

God is always listening. And it is God's loving care and
ceaseless attention that has empowered us each to live a
good life. We are humbled by his steadfastness and the
way he listens and responds to our prayers. Each of us is
a much blessed child of God.

December 19

Then said the prophet Jeremiah unto Hananiah the prophet,
Hear now, Hananiah; The Lord hath not sent thee;
but thou makest this people to trust in a lie.

—Jeremiah 28:15

Dear God, in times of stress or even of great abundance, I sometimes feel pulled to easy and gratifying answers. It's hard work to live in your word and to always remember to give credit where credit is due. Let me emulate Jeremiah's strength and judgment in calling out false prophets and upholding your word with my actions. Amen.

December 20

The Lord killeth, and maketh alive: he bringeth down to
the grave, and bringeth up. The Lord maketh poor, and
maketh rich: he bringeth low, and lifteth up.
—1 Samuel 2:6–7

Who among us hasn't stood at the top of a
scenic overlook and wondered at how far the world
extends in every direction? We
know that everything we see is
God's creation, but we don't
always see so much of that
creation in one view. Everything
we touch, he has touched
before. We are cushioned by
his love and awesome power
everywhere we look.

December 21

And the Lord said unto him, Peace be unto thee;
fear not: thou shalt not die.

—Judges 6:23

I believe in the sun even when it does not shine, and revel in the sunlight when it does emerge. I believe in love even when I do not feel it, and draw my loved ones to me when we are reunited. I believe in God even when he is silent, and feel the constant comfort of his eternal love in every step I take.

December 22

And it came to pass, when the ark set forward, that Moses
said, Rise up, Lord, and let thine enemies be scattered;
and let them that hate thee flee before thee.

— Numbers 10:35

Real love is not isolating. It opens doors, opens
horizons, and opens your heart. Search for people who
add to your life, who give you more than you would have
without them. Let those who would take away from your
growth and happiness find their way to the exit.

December 23

Now therefore put away, said he, the strange gods which are among you, and incline your heart unto the Lord God of Israel.

—Joshua 24:23

Listen to the sparrow's song. It's soft and serene like a breeze whistling through the woods or the gurgling of a brook. It's an angelic song that resonates with heaven's voice. Let the simple life take you by the hand today, and seek the goodness that only God can put in your heart. Be blessed and warmed in his life-giving presence!

December 24

And I will raise me up a faithful priest, that shall do according to that which is in mine heart and in my mind; and I will build him a sure house; and he shall walk before mine anointed for ever.

—1 Samuel 2:35

Loving you has been my greatest investment, Lord. For all the love I've given you, you've matched it 100 percent and paid interest in the form of guidance, security, encouragement, and joy. Thank you.

December 25

And Joshua said unto the people, Ye are witnesses against yourselves that ye have chosen you the Lord, to serve him. And they said, We are witnesses.

—Joshua 24:22

When we live with a heart of compassion, we have the heart of an angel. When we fill our lives with deeds of compassion, we do the work of an angel. These gestures shore up our love for and accountability to God. Joshua is right: we are our own best judges of how we are best able to serve the Lord, and we must answer to ourselves first and foremost for our actions.

December 26

The Lord lift up his countenance upon thee, and give thee peace. And they shall put my name upon the children of Israel, and I will bless them.

—Numbers 6:26–27

God, today I thank you for my wonderful family. My mom is my mom even though her children are grown up, on their own, and parents of their own kids. Her nurturing spirit didn't go away—-it lives on forever. I am blessed by her love and willingness to share her lifetime of wisdom.

December 27

*And Hannah prayed, and said, My heart rejoiceth in the Lord,
mine horn is exalted in the Lord: my mouth is enlarged over
mine enemies; because I rejoice in thy salvation.*

—1 Samuel 2:1

Sometimes we feel God isn't listening, though we
know in our hearts that he is. Hannah explains the truth
that we know: God lifts up our voices and hears them as
clear as day. When we believe in him, he gives us the same
priority we give
to him. There is
no hold music on
the line to God.

December 28

That ye may remember, and do all my commandments,
and be holy unto your God.

—Numbers 15:40

God promises many rewards to those who follow him with their faith and acts, but we can never forget that his standards are high. We must ask ourselves every day if we are honoring God with everything we have. And striving to uphold those high standards will make us better friends, neighbors, colleagues, and families.

December 29

*Have not I commanded thee? Be strong and of a good courage;
be not afraid, neither be thou dismayed: for the Lord thy God
is with thee whithersoever thou goest.*

—Joshua 1:9

Those closest to us will allow us to hold onto our dreams. That's why the first person who told you there is no Santa Claus was not your best friend! Our dreams of a life with God are real, and we are surrounded with signs of his presence. God's love is broad and vast and his dream of eternal life has already come true for us. We must only accept it.

December 30

And the children of Israel said unto the Lord, We have sinned;
do thou unto us whatsoever seemeth good unto thee;
deliver us only, we pray thee, this day.

—Judges 10:15

Each dawning of another day is a new opportunity to seek forgiveness from God. We rise and say a prayer that God will bless and keep us despite our flaws. God loves his children even when they don't seem to deserve it, and he offers every opportunity for us to do "whatsoever seemeth good unto thee."

December 31

For this child I prayed; and the Lord hath given me my petition which I asked of him: Therefore also I have lent him to the Lord; as long as he liveth he shall be lent to the Lord. And he worshipped the Lord there.

—1 Samuel 1:27–28

Thank you, loving God, for my mother with whom I share a connection to my own children. As Hannah gave Samuel as tribute in thanks for God's blessings, my mother raised us in the light of your love. She set an example I was grateful to follow with my own young family.

PHOTO CREDITS: